P9-DMU-315

LETTERS TO MY DAUGHTERS

Letters

TO MY

Daughters

THE *Art*
OF BEING A *Wife*

BARBARA RAINEY

BETHANYHOUSE

a division of Baker Publishing Group
Minneapolis, Minnesota

© 2016 by Barbara Rainey

Published by Bethany House Publishers
11400 Hampshire Avenue South
Bloomington, Minnesota 55438
www.bethanyhouse.com

Bethany House Publishers is a division of
Baker Publishing Group, Grand Rapids, Michigan

Printed in China

All rights reserved. No part of this publication may be reproduced, stored in a retrieval system, or transmitted in any form or by any means—for example, electronic, photocopy, recording—without the prior written permission of the publisher. The only exception is brief quotations in printed reviews.

ISBN 978-0-7642-1773-9

Library of Congress Control Number: 2015950819

Golden Pine copyright Makoto Fujimura/Fujimura Institute. Image used by permission.

"Dancing in the Minefields" written by Andrew Peterson, copyright © 2010 Jakedog Music (admin. by Music Services). All rights reserved. Used by permission.

Unless otherwise indicated, Scripture quotations are from The Holy Bible, English Standard Version® (ESV®), copyright © 2001 by Crossway, a publishing ministry of Good News Publishers. Used by permission. All rights reserved. ESV Text Edition: 2007

Scripture quotations identified NASB are from the New American Standard Bible®, copyright © 1960, 1962, 1963, 1968, 1971, 1972, 1973, 1975, 1977, 1995 by The Lockman Foundation. Used by permission.

Scripture quotations identified NIV are from the Holy Bible, New International Version®. NIV®. Copyright © 1973, 1978, 1984, 2011 by Biblica, Inc.™ Used by permission of Zondervan. All rights reserved worldwide. www.zondervan.com

Scripture quotations identified NKJV are from the New King James Version. Copyright © 1982 by Thomas Nelson, Inc. Used by permission. All rights reserved.

To protect the privacy of those outside the author's immediate family, some names and nonessential details have been changed.

Cover and interior design by Jennifer Parker
Cover art and interior hand-lettering by Corey Powell, Rogers, Arkansas
Contibuting art direction by Paul Higdon and LaVonne Downing

Author is represented by Wolgemuth & Associates

16 17 18 19 20 21 22   7 6 5 4 3 2

This book is dedicated to

Marsha Kay Rainey

Who, on the eve of her wedding, asked if I would share
some of what I have learned about being a wife.
It was never intended to be a book, of course, just letters,
sharing lessons of failures and triumphs,
for encouragement and hope.

May you, my sweet daughter-in-love,
hear love, always love, in these words.

*"We look not to the things that are seen
but to the things that are unseen.
For the things that are seen are transient,
but the things that are unseen
are eternal."*

2 Corinthians 4:18

And for
my daughters,

Ashley, Stephanie, Marsha Kay,
Rebecca, Deborah, and Laura

and all your friends,
dear gifts of God to you and to me

I love them for loving you:
Lincoln, Sarah, Katherine, Kate, Maggie, Amy, Beth, Margaret,
Ann, Emily, Sara, Andrea, Clara, Hanna, Elizabeth, Christy,
Kacey, Sheri, Natalie, Betsy, Johanna, Amy, Karthi, Teresa,
Brett, Christa, Kathryn, Janeen,
Marissa, Beth, Anjanette, Ellen,
and many more, including new friends I have yet to meet.

For my sweet young friends
Korie, Carrie, Janel, Erin, Kathryn, Tracy, Julie,
and all my reader friends who filled my inbox
with great feedback to my survey.

For you, your friends, and all daughters of Eve,
May these lessons learned give you encouragement and vision
to create with abandon in your marriages
that all may see the image of the Invisible
the hope of redemption
and the beauty of God's magnificent design for your union.

May your married love draw many to see Jesus.

Contents

An Open Letter to Daughters Everywhere

Dear Daughters,

Across the landscape of time, women have depended on other women for answers to the questions we all face. We've bravely asked one another about husbands and children, about work and worth, about cooking and cleaning, about friendships, finances, fears, and failures. And if we found ourselves in a time and place without anyone we could ask, we found that we were a bit lonely, a bit lost.

Mary, a young teen about to become a very young mother, went to her cousin Elizabeth's house to seek comfort and wisdom. She stayed for three months. We can only imagine the questions she asked, the conversations they had. And I wonder, *Why didn't Mary ask her own mother?* Or did she? Did Mary run to Elizabeth because her own mother couldn't get past the out-of-wedlock pregnancy and personal disgrace to really be there for her daughter? To listen to her thoughts and questions and fears? Or was it because Mary knew only Elizabeth could relate to her experience of carrying a child anointed by God?

There are some things you just can't talk to your mother about. So you talk to sisters, friends, other women who are older, wiser, and more experienced in life. Someone safer. I will freely admit my girls are cautious with their questions to me, and they should be. Women help each other find the right paths, and I would never want to be their only confidante.

Several years ago I took four of my six daughters and daughters-in-law away on a weekend without husbands and children. On the last night, as we were getting ready for bed, the three married girls started talking about sex. It was decided that they'd all meet in one bedroom and talk. They did not exclude me, but I knew the conversation would be different if I was there. So I excused myself and went to bed. Sometimes we need peers; sometimes we need someone older and wiser. I get that.

In 2001 I began this book as a series of email letters in response to sweet Marsha Kay's request for my advice on marriage. I included all my married daughters: Ashley, Marsha Kay (married to son Ben), and Stephanie (married to son Samuel). My goal was to encourage them as they began their marriages and were learning what it meant to be called *wife*. I hoped to impart some small doses of wisdom I'd acquired in my then three decades of marriage. More importantly, I wanted to give them a vision for the value gained from a lifetime of marital fidelity.

Since then, Dennis and I have celebrated our forty-first anniversary, and we've seen two more daughters, Rebecca and Deborah, marry. Laura, our youngest, is waiting her turn, and what a party it will be!

When my mother was a young bride in a faraway state, she was part of a round-robin letter with six or seven other women from back home. She always looked forward to seeing the thick legal envelope in the mailbox,

> I long to put the experience of fifty years at once into your young lives, to give you at once the key to that treasure chamber every gem of which has cost me tears and struggles and prayers, but you must work for these inward treasures yourselves.
>
> —Harriet Beecher Stowe

for it contained letters from each woman in the group. She read them all, enjoying each touch with that woman's life. Then she removed her original letter, wrote a new one to the group, and sent the packet on its way to the next woman in line. For my six girls and their friends and anyone else who wants to listen in, welcome to this "round robin" of my original letters, plus many inspired by more recent questions from young wives not biologically tied to me, but still in my heart.

I've included questions presented as though posed by one of my daughters. These are not specific questions from any of my girls, but rather compilations from hundreds of conversations with married women of all ages.

I invite you, any woman who wants to create beauty in her marriage, to read these letters and see if my journey might provide you courage and hope. Just as no woman pretends to have all the answers, neither do I. Any good within these pages is what God, as the divine Author, has written through me. It is His work I share. As my mother used to do when the much-anticipated letters arrived, I hope you can set aside your work for an hour, pour a fresh cup of coffee, and read a few letters at a time as if they were written for you alone.

May you be encouraged, strengthened, and inspired, dear daughter, to see a vision of what God might create in your own unique marriage.

Sent with love,
Barbara

CHAPTER 1

To my daughters everywhere,

One morning in May I began collecting. From the bookshelves in the living room, the bedroom, and my laundry room/office, I gathered all my books on marriage, old journals, and several newer books I had just ordered. After piling them in stacks on the coffee table, I sat on the couch with pens, Post-It notes, and my coffee to begin awakening memories. I wanted to gather for you all that has been helpful to me on being a wife, pivotal lessons learned from the land of "I do." I began with the oldest book, received as a wedding gift—its pink cover faded, its pages frayed and soft and heavily underlined, and its title still relevant: *To Have and To Hold* by Jill Renich (Zondervan, 1972).

Off to the side was a book I'd just ordered that had nothing to do with marriage. It was about art. All morning it beckoned to me, calling me to hurry and finish my work so I could enjoy its play. Like the promise of a treat to a child, its beautiful cover kept catching my eye, but I resisted to stay on task. Finally it was noon. I picked up the candy, Makoto Fujimura's book *Refractions*. Almost immediately I was enjoying the sweetness: the paintings, his reflections on beauty, his call to create.

"A Parable of Roots," the fourth essay, spoke not a word about marriage, but explored the making of Mako's painting *Golden Pine*. As I studied the image in the book and read his words of description, I was surprised and delighted to discover that this painting does in fact express relational truth. In *Golden Pine* I saw an image of marriage. It summarized something I want you, my daughters, to know.

Golden Pine is simply an enormous painting. It is 16.5 feet x 22.5 feet in size, and executed with pure mineral pigments and more than two thousand sheets of gold leaf applied to Japanese handmade paper. *Sounds a lot like marriage,* I thought as I read the descriptive words *handmade* and *labor-intensive*. The longer I studied the image, the more it spoke to me.

You've glanced at the painting, but look again. A secure tree reaching heavenward is the kind of wife I want to be—strong, always growing upward toward the One who made me and outward toward those He gave me to love and shelter. Now count the panels. Nine large panels make up the whole image, each one necessary for the overall effect, yet each an incomplete work if removed from the whole. The separate panels represent so much of the complexity of marriage. Each panel must work with the others to create the finished image of *Golden Pine*. So, too, as a wife, I must work in a multifaceted way in my marriage. Some situations where I function as a wife call for empathy and silence, and some for strong yet kind words of truth. Sometimes I help my husband in practical, tangible ways; sometimes I help by backing off; and sometimes I help with words that are a gentle nudging, a reminder, an encouragement to keep trusting.

Just as one panel of the painting features roots, and another the trunk, I see my life in pieces, too: as helper and lover, one who respects, believes, and trusts. Yet all must work together, connected, intertwined daily—like the roots of a tree that dig into the ground and the limbs on the branches

---

Photo opposite page: *Golden Pine* by Makoto Fujimura

that forever twirl and twist outward. The panels of *Golden Pine* work together to create a complete image. Marriage is to be like this painting: strong, growing, multifaceted, richly developed, and reflecting

God wants marriages to inspire wonder in those who are close enough to see the radiant beauty only He can create.

the Light of its Creator.

Which reminds me of an important truth about marriage. I've not seen the actual painting of *Golden Pine*, since it hangs in Hong Kong. Someday perhaps. But viewing this reproduction seems so much like viewing any marriage from afar. We do not know the depth of beauty and grace in the marriages around us. Nor can we see in other marriages what the Artist might have done if not stopped by unbelief. But to see God create and rescue and redeem in my marriage is like the experience of seeing a Mako masterpiece up close, which

I have in New York City. His work is stunning and seems to glow from within as if touched by the Light of heaven. So, too, God wants my marriage and yours to inspire wonder in those who are close enough to see the radiant beauty only He can create.

How I want this for my marriage and yours—not only to see God's design clearly but to experience His gifts deeply. Both husbands and wives are imperfect humans, and we often have a difficult time blending all aspects of our lives in a balanced way. I've often felt the need to focus on one aspect of my life so that I can get it right (I always tend to think there is a "right" way), but in doing so I neglect other areas. In Mako's painting I see how each panel, like each function in marriage, is important and not interchangeable. When Mako was creating *Golden Pine*, he worked on all nine panels simultaneously so that what he executed on the lower left panel connected to the panel to the right and the one above. He had to keep the whole in mind while working on each individual piece.

We must do the same as wives. My gifts and my responsibilities in marriage cannot be isolated one from the other. It is part of the challenge and the mystery of marriage—how we cooperate with God, who designed us for this, remembering it is He "who is at work in you" to create a relationship of great beauty worthy of His glory.

Marriage, like painting or any of a million other creative ventures, requires time, money, energy, and effort along with ever-present risk. *What if this idea doesn't work as I envisioned it? What if it is not received?* Many great artists have had their work criticized, marred, and even rejected. So, too, has God. His intricately

Our marriages are meant to be statements of wonder to the watching world, statements of the goodness, the power, the beauty of God.

crafted union of male and female also posed a risk of significant proportions. He knew marriages would fail, that His hoped-for plans of glory would not all be as He envisioned. Many see His design as if it were diabolical, a piece of art they find ugly. They don't see the loveliness of His Word to us, of His names for us, and instead call them restrictive and distorted. Even those of us who welcome God's plan for marriage are often bewildered by some of the elements He adds to His chosen form. We question submission. We resent our differences. Rather than trust the Master Artist, the Supreme Designer, we critique his masterpiece, as if we know better. Yet with each pigment, each stroke, each design feature, God is speaking to the watching world about His character and love. Marriage is a mystery we will not unravel.

Marriage is so worth fighting for, so worth keeping and enjoying, giving oneself to completely. For God has planted marriage in every culture so that His message of love can be seen in unions of beauty generation after generation.

Just as we look with awe at *Golden Pine* and think, *Wow, how did he do that? I can't imagine,* so our marriages are meant to be statements of wonder to the watching world, statements of the goodness, the power, and the beauty of God. My fascination with this painting leads me to want to know Mako the artist himself, to learn from him, to see his talent up close. And so it is that admiring a beautifully mature marriage makes us want to know both the couple

and the Creator. And that is the eternal purpose for marriage, making Him known.

As we talk together about being a wife, it's so important that we keep the big picture in mind. So as you keep reading, remember:

- Marriage is an unfathomable mystery with hidden rewards to be discovered together.

- Though there is a form to be followed by faith, there isn't a foolproof formula.

- Come with an open heart, unafraid to hear the whispers of heaven.

Love and prayers,
Mom

Image above: *Artist in the Simplon,* watercolor, by John Singer Sargent.
Courtesy of the Fogg Houat of Art.

MYSTERY

An idea conceived
Before Adam and Eve,
Before Days, Stars and Nights
Before Darkness and Light.
Belov'd Splendor rebelled.
Cruel mutiny. Quelled.
Lo, betrayal divorced
Divine Love, rent by force.

Three in One then imagined
Fresh canvas and passion,
For Beauty, her Man:
A new story began.
Designed to show oneness
Create pure abundance.
Heav'ns hope now revived
Holy Sabbath arrived.
A dark shadow too shrewd,
Sly sin lied, trust unglued.
Not betrayal again!
When will rebellion end?

Witness thousands of years
Wedded joys and sad tears,
Watching gazes of angels
will these two be faithful?
The manger, the cross
Rescued, set free those lost.
Will my union reflect
His joy to resurrect?

Spirit, my Guide
Restore me, as His bride
To believe every word
Of the song yet unheard.
Our creation to be
Like Thee, O Trinity
Create, sculpt, refine
Me, my Savior divine.
Our marriage reflection
A pleasing redemption.
May we plant, paint and sing
Together for the King.

—Barbara Rainey

Marriage
IS LIKE
Fine
Cuisine

CHAPTER 2

The last time I kept Ashley's five boys, the older two were eager to demonstrate for me their newly acquired ability to "cook." Firstborn Samuel carefully followed the directions for the boxed mac and cheese while second-born James scared me to death by casually standing right next to a boiling pan of water, waiting for the go-ahead to pour in the noodles. I refrained from telling them to "be careful," but instead gave generous praise I didn't taste the final product. Luckily, they were more enamored than I with the end result . . . eagerly inhaling it themselves.

They were justifiably proud. But was it really cooking? Well, it depends. My grandsons called it cooking, but let's face it . . . there's a big difference between mac and cheese and beef Wellington.

Famous chef Julia Child had recipes that called for the finest, freshest ingredients in precise quantities, added in sequential steps with exact cooking times. Julia was known for generous simmering, melding nuanced flavors, and correct blending, folding, and mixing, all to create deliciousness in every bite, from main course to dessert. She cooked an *experience,* not just food to fill stomachs, and she awakened in legions of followers a desire to think of cooking on a level far beyond boxed mac and cheese.

Like continuing to eat kid food after we've become adults, our marriages can fail to develop the mature experience of fine cuisine when we become weary and quit trying. Too often, married couples settle for only elementary grades of cooking when difficult challenges, like complicated recipes, are not mastered with the first attempt. Perseverance is required to learn the skill of a professional chef. And a good teacher can show the way to master the basics.

I don't know about you, but I want magic in my marriage. I want the raw, chopped, incomplete ingredients I bring to the kitchen transformed into satisfying goodness. I want the joy of experiencing fine cuisine all the way to the end. Do you?

EMBRACING YOUR DIFFERENCES

Cooking With Different Cookbooks

Dear Mom,

Honestly, we did great for the first few months—we were all about life together and thought our differences added a spark to our lives. Now we both seem to be withdrawing, staking ground for ourselves rather than growing together. How did you and Dad embrace your differences rather than let them pull you apart?

Dear daughters,

Here's my story, and a little background to help set the stage. I think you'll see I've been there, too.

One of my early dates with Dennis was on a warm Saturday afternoon in June in Dallas. He picked me up in his light blue Chevy Impala and drove us out in the country for fishing and a picnic. (Our very *first* date was for a proper lunch, thankfully, for I had never been around smelly fish and bait in my life. He might have lost me had he begun there.) Dennis grew up with a fishing pole as an extension of his arm. It's amazing what a girl will do when she is falling in love. Like skiing down black-diamond slopes in the Canadian Rockies, Rebecca? Or getting blistered feet from hiking, right, Ashley?

Fishing was just the beginning of many adventures in a whole new world that opened before me when I accepted this young man's proposal of marriage. The new experiences after I said "I do" kept me wide-eyed with wonder for many of those early years. Like Alice who fell through the rabbit hole and woke up in a world that was familiar but oh so different, I found myself not just seeing trees, but sleeping under them; not just looking up at snow-covered mountains, but also flying down them with long skinny things strapped to my boots; not just admiring bubbling streams, but learning the names of the fish that swam beneath and would hopefully end up on the line of my new husband's fly rod. (And by the way, in case you haven't learned this yet, a fly rod is different from a rod and reel. Who knew?) I even learned to help cook a fair number of dead fish over a fire at our many campsites.

Dennis wasn't just different. His recipe for life was positively *foreign*. We were like oil and water, constantly separating in our jar. We cannot be more different. (Notice I switched to present tense!)

I remember Dennis would get an idea and be off and running. I, on the other hand, was used to thinking things through and evaluating what to do before acting. Often, during our first year of marriage, I felt left in the dust.

Dennis was expressive and always asking questions; I tended to be quiet and cautious, thinking about what I wanted to say before I said it. I felt overexposed.

And then there was money. Dennis wanted to spend money on fishing; I wanted to spend money on furniture. We had a combined income, but how did we determine who spent what? I felt it unfair that he freely spent what he wanted when he wanted without consulting me. I felt confused.

It sounds like you are facing something similar. Adjustments are awkward. And the early years of marriage are full of adjustments, always more than any couple ever anticipates! As our family friend Lincoln discovered when her new husband wanted to "debate" everything! He has a quick, active intellect and loved playing devil's advocate and challenging her thinking. She felt defensive and on trial. And then he couldn't understand why she couldn't act "fine" and snuggle up on the couch after they finished "talking"! He also could not understand why she, from a family of four girls, expected to go shopping at the beginning of each season for a few new additions to her wardrobe.

The unique, fresh traits that attracted

Choose to believe that his differences are for your good. And yours are good for him, too.

Although day-to-day married life may seem as natural and almost as automatic as breathing, yet there is a way in which the two partners never really
do get used to one another, not in the way they are used to breathing.

—Mike Mason, *The Mystery of Marriage*

us to our spouses while dating will become tiresome
or irritating after years, or even just months, of marriage. When I encounter (note the present-tense verb
again) these clashes, I have learned I have choices.
Do I communicate disdain for a trait I feel is flawed?
Will I withdraw to avoid dealing with it? Should I try
to change him? Do we talk about it? The challenge
of mixing the ingredients of his personality and mine
was just beginning in those early years.

When you went to culinary school, Rebecca, I was
fascinated to learn from you the endless possibilities for
creativity in cooking. You taught me that we eat with
our eyes first (presentation is important), and that there
are great subtleties of flavor in different salts, vinegars,
and olive oils. You taught me that when baking, salt
balances the sweet ingredients and causes their flavors
to come alive. Even the freshness of cream, butter, and
Parmesan cheese is enhanced with salt. I had no idea.

It reminds me of Jesus saying, "You are the salt
of the earth." Which raises these questions: "Does my
husband's life taste better with me in it?" "Is the salt
of my life overpowering, or just enough to enhance
the sweetness in our union?" "Will I allow his unique
version of salt to bring out a better flavor in me?"

Differences. The first and most lasting surprise in
marriage. It was easy in the beginning—accepting
and enjoying the differences that attracted us to each

other. But now, the everyday clash of those differences must be met with a decision to once again accept the other person as God's gift to you. You were confident when engaged that he was perfect for you, right? So now it's time to ask God to help you see him as you once did. He will mellow over time, but until then, choose to believe that his differences are for your good. And yours are good for him, too.

Remember:

- Each marriage brings unique ingredients unlike any other couple's combination. Every union is a one-of-a-kind creation.

- Differences are good and normal. Welcome them.

- Feeling surprised by them is normal, too; relax in the process.

- How you respond is totally in your control.

More to come,
Mom

RESTATING THE TRUTH
The Bookend Recipe

Dear Mom,

Okay, I get that we're supposed to embrace our differences, and why. Obviously I want that, more than anyone. But what do you do when things you once thought were cute aren't so cute anymore? What do I do when he is now just irritating me? I need to try something!

Dear daughters,

One of your dad's favorite quotes is "Love is blind, but marriage is an eye-opener." It's an old standby because it always gets a laugh. But the laughter reveals the universal truth everyone recognizes. Reality sets in when those unique qualities that initially attracted you now feel irritating and difficult. It's all about perspective.

Some of the differences I encountered were the ways we handled money, the ways we spent our free time, the ways we each expressed our emotions, the ways we each felt about sex. All were topics that needed discussion to achieve new levels of understanding. And we both soon learned they required more than just a one-time dialogue. A lifelong conversation was more like it. And they're still going on today. . . .

It's not only that we are different. How we express those differences create clashes. It's the clothes on the floor, the loudly shut doors, the toilet seat left up, the disaster left in *my* car, the moving of *my* stuff or the taking over of *my* space, the forgetting to call when he's late or forgetting to tell me about that meeting and no, he can't take the kids to practice. Or as one of you said to me, "He asks me to add things he needs done to my already-crazy-full day like I have nothing else to do!" Do I hear a scream?

Like misreading one teaspoon of salt as one tablespoon of salt, how we interpret his words or actions makes or ruins the recipe. When I interpret his clothes left on the floor as a message that says "You are my servant," I believe the worst. That thought never crossed my husband's mind. It was just a bad habit. (And one that can and should be corrected out of love; but these things take time!) From his perspective, my requests for him to pick up his clothes sounded to him like his mother, and he thought, *Can't I just be myself? What does it matter?* Like my friend MaryAnn said, "Dropping a towel on the floor is about a lot more than a dropped towel."

I've learned that successfully blending the ingredients of our lives takes years and years and years of practice. Not weeks or months. I am far too impatient—are you, too? Giving each other the benefit of the doubt is a choice love makes. Repeatedly. It means when the clothes or towels are left on the floor *again*, I choose to believe my husband did not *intentionally* neglect to

pick them up just to create more work for me. Believing the best means I don't misread his actions as a personal affront toward me. I also don't become arrogant and assume that just because I don't leave the floor trashed (in my humble opinion), I am superior to him. We're just different.

Since he and I are cooking in the same kitchen in life, we need to find ways to cooperate, to believe the best about each other, to invite conversation while we work at this pot of stew called marriage. The temptation—when a recipe calls for another seemingly impossible mixing of differences—is to give up in resignation or to quit the marriage entirely.

One of my favorite verses says "Nothing is impossible with God." It's helped me in countless moments of failure to not quit, but to review the divine instructions again—to initiate another conversation, perhaps this time in an atmosphere of love rather than accusation. To pull on the chef's coat and remember respect and honor. You and your husband are a team, chef and sous-chef. Believe the best, keep talking about your differences, and don't quit on that recipe! Deliciousness awaits, in time.

chef and sous-chef

You and your husband are a team, chef and sous-chef.
Believe the best, keep talking about your differences, and
don't quit on that recipe! Deliciousness awaits, in time.

Over the years I've acquired a stack of go-to recipes that always win: brisket, cheese grits, rice pudding, my grandmother's pound cake recipe, and many more. A no-fail marital recipe that we've used for years is the bookend principle. It's a recipe for sweetening those hard-to-swallow conversations. Just as bookends are used to prop up books that contain truth, so your dad and I have always spoken a verbal reminder of our love, loyalty, and complete acceptance at *both* ends of difficult discussions. Thousands of times over these forty years, we have gone back to the original recipe and said to each other, "I love you, and I'm committed to you. I will work this through with you so we can build a better marriage." The security of those bookends, affirming that we believe in the best for our marriage, has always made the difficult truth much easier to hear.

Consider these questions: "Am I more willing to give my girlfriend the benefit of the doubt than my husband?" "Is it easier to assume she didn't mean it than to believe my husband didn't mean it?" "Do I hold him to a higher standard?" "Why do I expect so much from him?"

My husband and yours need to frequently hear words of commitment and acceptance. And you do, too. Remind each other of your love. Tell him that you'd choose to marry him again. Tell him you are grateful for him. Thank him for making you laugh, for caring about your well-being, for trying hard, for going to work each day, for taking out the trash, for being spontaneous, for not quitting or giving up on you or your marriage. Find those positives and tell him what you like about him. Conversations about differences and areas of conflict are easier to process when supported by bookends of abundant love and encouragement.

Remember:

- Use the bookend recipe often.

- Believing the best is a choice. Make it often.

- And keep the conversations going. Never give up. Never stop talking.

Praying you will remember that nothing is too hard for God,
Mom

Ingredients That Never Blend

Dear Mom,

Thanks for the note. It really helped. We've tried the bookends recipe, and I know Dad will probably gloat when he finds out it's working for us, too. But here's the thing: Yeah, Dad irritates you in ten different ways. But I've never seen the kinds of things in your marriage like I have in mine. . . . There are a few things that really scare me, because I think they're unresolvable. And they could break us. What then?

My sweet girls,

First of all, what you've seen in our marriage isn't all there is. So I want to caution you: Just because you don't see the same scary struggles between your dad and me or in other couples doesn't mean we don't have equally challenging or even frightening issues. Second, *scary* can have a hundred different meanings. Is it scary that he has no interest in helping you with cleaning the apartment, or is it scary that you've discovered he's breaking the law in some way? There is a big difference. So for this letter I'm going to tackle the picky drive-you-crazy things and save the bigger sin issues for another letter.

This story is about a "smaller" impossibility, but I learned something important through this clash of differences. My first encounter with in-gredients that refused to blend was with the laundry. For a season of years in our marriage, this was a disagreement that felt irreconcilable.

Early in our marriage, I realized while doing the laundry that your dad's T-shirts, boxers, and socks were always inside out, and I always took

To love is not just to view someone as the most wonderful person in the world or as some kind of saint. It is also to see all the weakness, the false-ness and shoddiness, all the very worst in the loved one exposed—and then to be enabled, by the pure grace of God, not only to accept this person, but to accept in a deeper, more perfect way than was possible before. . . . Before love can really begin to be love, it must face and forgive the very worst in the person loved.

—Mike Mason, *The Mystery of Marriage*

the extra time to turn them right side out and then fold them. So I asked him one day why he took his clothes off that way and if he could change the way he undressed so my chore would be easier.

He answered, "That's the way I've always done it." He wasn't angry at all. Flippant was more like it. Dismissive. Like many men, he may have thought I just wanted the facts. Or it's possible that my tone was whiny or critical, or maybe my timing was off. Bad timing in baking a cake can ruin it, just as it can ruin marital conversations. Those are details I don't remember. I did continue to fold his clothes, turning them all right side out for years and years. Yes, yes . . . I can hear you now. No, it never occurred to me to fold them inside out or to not fold them at all. And I know in today's marriages many men do their own laundry. But this is my story, and I wasn't into confrontation.

But about ten years later, now facing laundry for *eight* people, I decided to ask again. I was desperate to save any time I could. This time I explained that it wasn't a deal breaker for our marriage, but with all I had to do, it would be really helpful if he would

You are each a Gift to the other. You are each God's handmade Work of Art designed by Him for one another.

change the way he'd "always" taken his clothes off. And he agreed. No big discussion. No big deal. Done. I was surprised, but by then both of us had matured. I learned that timing matters, and that changing habits takes time. By this season of our lives he had learned the importance of noticing all I was managing and wanted to serve me. He wanted to lighten my load and made it a point to co-operate for my sake. It was a reminder to me of the value of waiting, of being patient, of not making an issue out of everything. All in God's timing—there really is power in trusting in that.

The famous Serenity Prayer says "God, grant me the grace to accept with serenity the things I cannot change, courage to change the things which should be changed, and the wisdom to distinguish the one from the other." These words were cross-stitched and hanging in Grandmother Rainey's house, but I dismissed them as a sappy sentiment. But the truth is there is much that cannot be changed in your husband, just as there is much in you that cannot be changed. It is the wise woman who accepts that fact and trusts God to do any changing on His timetable.

A good friend of ours, Tim Muehlhoff, told your dad and me about a survey he found that helped his marriage. The study found that the majority of conflicts couples deal with cannot be fully resolved and will be with a couple in one form or another for the life of the marriage. Here's the best part: The reason these conflicts are ongoing is that neither person is wrong concerning the issue, because most of these disagreements start with fundamental differences of lifestyle, personality, or values.

Did you hear that? In most repeated conflicts, neither spouse is wrong. It's simply a matter of differences in your values or personalities. It would have helped me to know it decades ago. Does that relieve you, too?

You may be thinking, *He doesn't know what I have to deal with.* Which is exactly the point. Every marriage has significant, unique differences to which you must respond with grace and love or allow them to divide you. Learning to be at peace with our different preferences has been liberating. As Dennis has said so many times, "Different isn't wrong, it's just different." (Quit rolling your eyes. There's truth in that.)

Everyone knows changing each other isn't the goal of marriage, though you and your husband will repeatedly make this mistake over the length of your marriage. I hope you can see that differences aren't the real issue. Again, it is your response that matters. The temptation is to think in terms of who is right and who is wrong, or whose way is better, when mistakes are made.

Too often couples allow differences to create distance instead of deliberately celebrating each other as unique creations of God. Most of us married because we identified qualities or characteristics in our spouse that complemented or completed us. It would be good if you reminded each other in those difficult moments that you are each a gift to the other. And even more, you are each God's

handmade work of art designed by Him for one another. "Whatever is true, whatever is honorable . . .
think about these things" (Philippians 4:8). Focus on
the good.

And someday as you continue cooking and growing
together, you will come to a place where you appreciate and even love the unusual ingredients he brings to
your life. It's who he is.

Remember:

- Timing is critical in resolving differences. Be patient while you wait. Brace yourself for years of
  waiting, even a lifetime with some differences,
  trusting the God who created you both and
  brought you together.

- Ask Him for a dose of His gracious love. I have
  asked God to give me His love many, many times.
  Mine just isn't adequate.

- And don't compare your marriage with other
  marriages. Give thanks for your man and keep
  cooking!

With greater grace for all,
Mom

Cooking Times Vary

Refined taste. It comes with age, like a fine wine. Gone are the days of hot dogs, pizza, macaroni and cheese, and other kid food. Paul said, "When I became a man, I did away with childish things" (1 Corinthians 13:11 NASB). Of course, he wasn't referring to food choices, but the point is that when we grow up, we set aside the inferior for the superior. In our marriage today, love matters more than who is right or wrong.

But we didn't get to this place easily or quickly. Hundreds of times we re-discussed the way we load the dishwasher, our different methods of relating to our kids, or how we approach sex. Even though we are now at the finishing-each-other's-sentences stage of marriage, I am still realizing there is more to learn about this man to whom I am still married.

Vast differences still remain.

He still misplaces things and asks me if I've seen them. It used to bug me because I felt he was implying I should be like his mother and keep track of all his stuff! He wasn't. They were only simple questions that I misinterpreted with suspicion. Misreading the recipe again. My bad, not his.

He still thinks randomly; I still think sequentially.

He still thinks globally; I still think locally.

He is still more spontaneous; I am still a type-A planner.

He will always be a people person; I will always be wired to think about tasks.

He still loves new adventures, and I still hesitate initially, but then I usually go and love it.

He has been so good for me in so many ways. And I've been good for him, too.

Two summers ago while we were hiking in Telluride, Colorado, Dennis said to me as I stopped to catch my breath, "Let's hike to the top of that ridge."

I answered, "You've got to be kidding!" (We were already at an elevation of over ten thousand feet.)

"Come on," he said. "It's not that far."

My mind said, *It looks way too far for me,* but what came out of my mouth was, "Okay." As we started uphill, I added, "Do you realize that this hike is a picture of our marriage? You've been leading me to places unknown for decades. I keep following a few paces behind, trying to keep up with your sense of adventure."

He agreed and said, "Correct. My leading and your resisting, but coming along anyway!" We laughed, enjoying the sweet goodness. Some things truly never change.

But a few things *have* changed. He has learned to appreciate and enjoy art and has lovingly gone to many a museum with me. He has learned to shop, graciously giving me his time and not complaining, even spoiling me many times. He has even learned to garden. His mother would be shocked.

In turn, I have learned to appreciate hunting. I actually went with him on an elk hunt a few years ago, fully outfitted with the camo, face paint, and human-scent killer sprayed on my body! Aren't you impressed? We hiked and hiked and then snuck up on this herd of elk, hiding behind trees like we were clandestine spies following a double agent down a dark alley in Eastern Europe! It was truly fun.

My wonderful husband is gentler, kinder, and more compassionate toward me than ever. He has apologized many times for the immature things he did and said in our early years as we've had time to relive some of our early days, marveling that we stuck together. And I have apologized in return for my mistakes, which are legion. I

Our differences are
exactly the ingredients
God wanted to use
to grow each of us into a better
reflection
OF HIS image.

am much more open and honest and lighthearted than when we were first married. He teases that I am now the more expressive one in our marriage.

I'm beginning to believe he's right.

It's a wonderful thing about God's will and work that we'll never understand: how God takes two people and uses them both in each other's lives to grow the other into a more complete picture of what He intended. Like baking a delicious cake. Or the art of aging a fine wine or the best balsamic vinegar. The process cannot be rushed, or the end result will be either ruined or mediocre. Patience is essential, and both your generation and mine are short on that godly quality.

Our differences have generated a lot of friction over the years, but they are exactly the ingredients God wanted to use to grow each of us into a better reflection of His image. It is His goal for us to be more like Christ, and marriage is one of His favorite processes for accomplishing that end. It reminds me of Philippians 2:13: "For it is God who is at work in you, both to will and to work for His good pleasure" (NASB).

I hope our story of continued growth and change will comfort you, dear daughters, regardless of what you face. Differences *can* feel impossible, and even though many will never go away, God can still create beauty and joy in your marriage. So embrace your differences. See them as gifts from God to expand your understanding of Him and His design for your life. He makes no mistakes.

Our own baking is almost complete. We are having our cake and eating it, too. And it is a wonderfully

sweet season. If you asked us what kind of cake our marriage has become, Dennis would say it's a rich dark chocolate with piles of chocolate icing. I'd say it's a beautiful red velvet cake with a smooth cream cheese icing.

Different answers, of course, but both are right.

- The future is good.

- Anticipate it with hope and expectation

With love, always,
Mom

Marriage IS LIKE Grand Architecture

CHAPTER 3

One of my dreams as a mom was to show my children the beautiful cathedrals in France. In the summer of 2000, Dennis was booked to speak at a conference in Europe, so we took our son Samuel and our three youngest daughters with us. After the conference we rented two small cars (the six of us wouldn't fit in one) and took off to visit Chartres Cathedral. One of the most famous cathedrals in Europe, Chartres is breathtaking in its size and beauty. The sense of majesty and grandeur called our hearts to worship the One who is supreme.

Our next stop was Sainte-Chappelle in Paris. Smaller, but more elegant than its famous neighbor, Notre Dame, Sainte-Chappelle is a lapis jewel that sparkles with light flowing from tall, exquisite stained-glass windows that wordlessly speak of God's work. It was for us—and for any who visit—impossible to stand inside without lifting our eyes heavenward. Majestic cathedrals speak of the grandeur and grace of God, each uniquely proclaiming

Christ's life and the Bible's story.

At the end of our tours, however, I was left with a great feeling of sadness that many of the magnificent structures, masterpieces of architecture and beauty, are void of the Spirit for whom they were built. For centuries, many have been hollow and lifeless, mere museums, concert halls, and tourist attractions. But when the Spirit of Christ is welcomed within, any church can come back to life.

Marriages are like churches—some are grand in scale like cathedrals, while others more closely resemble a small country parish. The power of any church is not in its size, but in its people who are alive with the life of Christ. My marriage and yours must be filled with the Spirit of Christ, each spouse humbly following His leadership, if we want it to be all it was built to be. Then, like a church spire, our lives and the beauty of our marriage will irresistibly draw others in and point them to God, the Redeemer of our unique marriage story.

A ROCK-SOLID FOUNDATION

"I Surrender All"

Dear Mom,

So here's the deal. I thought we were really well matched when we got married—in our faith, that is—but I'm realizing we are really different here, too. It seems like we are doing well, and then out of the blue it feels like we are out of sync, or totally missing each other. It always catches me off guard. Advice?

My marriage and yours must be *filled with the Spirit of Christ,* each spouse humbly following His leadership, if we want it to be all it was built to be.

To my girls,

I do get how easy it is to miss one another. Still happens to us, too, from time to time. The key is to make sure you both stay securely anchored to the solid Bedrock of your lives, not unlike the enormous foundation stones underneath the ancient temple in Jerusalem and the rock supporting historic cathedrals. You need to keep your focus on your own heart and who you are becoming, and not on your husband. So here's more of my story:

Churches and cathedrals have witnessed countless weddings. I was twenty-three when I walked down the aisle and repeated "I do." To myself I thought, *I can do this, and I will be the best wife ever!* Did you feel that way, too, in your gown of white?

My confidence was high. My husband-to-be and I were committed Christ followers and not just Sunday-morning pew warmers—so matrimonial success was virtually guaranteed, right? I was sure we would build a great marriage together and that it would be relatively easy.

Okay, I *know* you felt that way, too! We all start out optimistic-to-the-max. Until reality crashes in.

I guess I should've told you that building a God-honoring marriage can be precarious, even scary at times. Sorry. Maybe then I should have tried to warn you, but you wouldn't have believed me any more than I would have believed it on my wedding day. Most work in marriage is on-the-job training. But I've learned it's not impossible even when it feels that way, so be encouraged.

You grew up singing about foundations. Remember? "The wise man built his house upon the rock." And now the tune will be stuck in your head! Maybe that is good. But I wonder about the man who built on the sand. What was he thinking? Was he trying to avoid the back-breaking pain of busting into the rock? Or did he think, "I can make this work; storms don't happen to the people I see living here."

Beginning is always the easiest part of a marriage, but also the most crucial. Like building a cathedral—the higher you climb on the scaffolding, the more clearly you can see if the walls are plumb or not. When you are missing one another, it means some of your building is not lined up squarely on the foundation stones.

I know you know the right foundation for your marriage is the Rock of Christ. But it's so much more than just believing that He exists, or knowing the creeds. It's belonging to Him as His daughter and being all His. It's taking Him at His word when He says He will supply all your needs or when He says to forgive, just as God in Christ has forgiven you. It's throwing yourself on Him because you have learned you simply cannot make this marriage thing that He created actually work. And then you do it all over again every time you feel out of sync. Sometimes it's needed daily.

Do you remember hearing us tell the story of our first Christmas, four months after our wedding? That December your dad and I signed over everything in our lives to God.

> God gives you Christ as the foundation of your marriage. "Welcome one another, therefore, as Christ has welcomed you, for the glory of God" (Rom. 15:7). . . . Don't insist on your rights, don't blame each other, don't judge or condemn each other, don't find fault with each other, but accept each other as you are, and forgive each other every day from the bottom of your hearts.
>
> —Dietrich Bonhoeffer

We both wrote letters to God giving Him our lives before we gave each other our first Christmas gifts. It was a way of saying, "You are first in our lives, God, and we want you to always be first." No one witnessed this little ceremony, but we hoped He would be pleased.

It seemed simple at the time—almost unnecessary, since we'd both given our lives to Christ years before—but in hindsight it was anything but insignificant. Given the trials and tests to come, it was pivotal. Jesus was the Cornerstone of our faith, but that first Christmas in 1972, He became the Cornerstone of our marriage.

My generation rebelled against ceremony, institutions, and denominational churches, many of us refusing to walk in graduation ceremonies or use traditional vows in our weddings. Similarly, it would be easy for your generation to regard our little Christmas ceremony as redundant and unnecessary. Old-fashioned. Quaint. After all, God knows you believe all that already, right? But surrender is the essence of the gospel, and sometimes an outward expression of that inward commitment makes a stronger foundation. "If we confess our sins, he is faithful and just to forgive us our sins and to cleanse us from all unrighteousness" (1 John 1:9).

And so, if you're struggling now, do a foundation inspection. Is Jesus the Cornerstone of your life? And your marriage? You might have asked Jesus into your heart when you were little, but now as a woman, there are more distractions, more to lure you away from your first love. An old hymn says, "Prone to wander, Lord, I feel it, prone to leave the God I love."

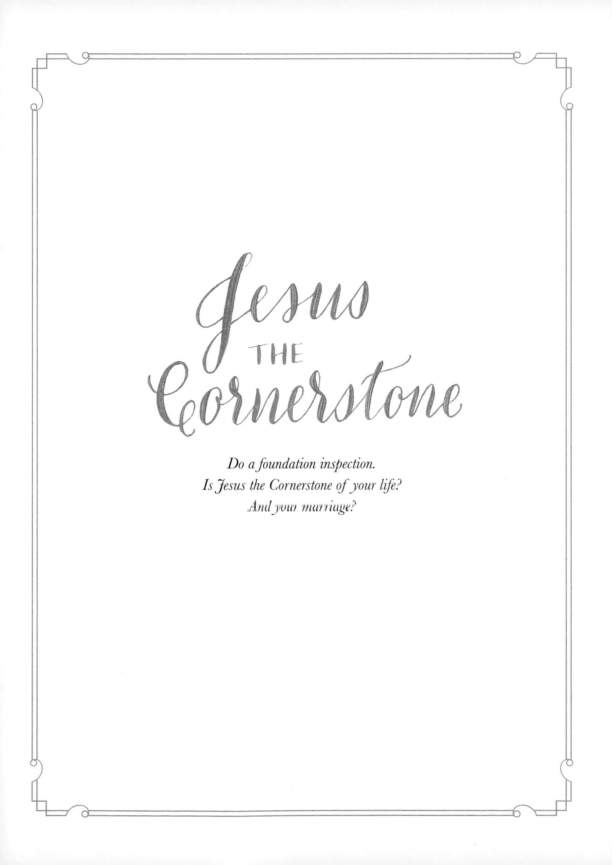

Jesus
THE
Cornerstone

Do a foundation inspection.
Is Jesus the Cornerstone of your life?
And your marriage?

Remember:

- Surrender to Jesus is not a one-time decision, but a daily one.

- A beautiful marriage is not possible without a solid foundation built on the Rock of Christ.

It's always a good time to make sure your heart is all His,
Mom

PRAYING FOR YOUR HUSBAND

Blueprints for a Chapel

Dear Mom,

I thought I could help him more, not really change him from who he is but, you know, help him get better at some stuff. Turns out, I can't. What now?

My daughters,

Ah yes, trying to change our husbands . . . something almost every married woman I know has wrestled—or still wrestles—with. You're in good company. And there is a way out.

When I was a new bride, I eagerly and expectantly jumped into learning to cook, fixing up our apartment, and doing life as a newlywed couple. As the months rolled along, I thought it my duty to help this husband of mine in some areas of his life. As I wrote in my letters on differences, I believed my orderly way of approaching life was superior to his spontaneous style.

It wasn't an arrogant attitude on my part as much as it was a naïve belief that my way seemed truly better. *Maybe his mother didn't train him well or show him how to be organized,* I thought. I assumed he simply needed my help to . . . change. I'm supposed to be his helper, right?

The solution was prayer, I decided. Aren't wives supposed to pray for their husbands? *I can do this* was my mantra. Dutifully, I recorded the things in Dennis that I thought needed refining. I was sure God would agree with me. It made so much sense! After a few weeks my list had grown to ten traits I now saw as weaknesses. To pray faithfully meant to do it daily, I thought, and I did. No one was going to call *me* a slacker wife.

But intently focusing on all these aspects of my husband that "needed repair" created another problem. Like the 300mm zoom lens on my camera, my prayers concentrated my gaze on only one side of my husband: the features I thought needed to be changed. Every day I repeated this list in fervent prayer, and that just made me notice them even more. It was as if my list were written on his back in bright neon ink.

To make it worse, God wasn't answering. Nothing was changing. I thought it was the "right" approach because it seemed "spiritual," but the result was that constantly noticing "flaws" took the joy out of our relationship. And so I decided to quit praying my list. I told the Lord that it was His business to change my husband's life. I said, "Lord, I give my husband to you, along with all these things that I think need to be changed or refined. If you want to change any of these in him, it's up to you. You are God and I am not." In hindsight, my requests were like trying to stop the wind. I was asking God to change His sovereign design for my husband's personality and wiring!

I tore up my list and threw it away, deciding to trust God with my husband's carefree approach to life, and to accept him as he was designed to be. I was not and am still not responsible for his life and how he lives it. Yes, those differences continued to cause me stress, and they still do, but God's creative genius trumped my preferences. After I resigned as architect of the Husband Remodeling Project, God changed my focus back to the big picture of the gift Dennis was to me. And in only days, I didn't notice the things that were wrong nearly as often. It was a great relief.

I had the responsibility about praying for my husband right, but my intent was amiss. I naïvely thought I was cooperating with God when I was actually trying to direct God to line up my husband with my ideals. Gently God showed me it wasn't about what *I* wanted, but what *He* wanted to do in my husband's life that mattered. After thinking about the situation for several weeks, I asked God what I should pray for. I didn't get an audible reply, but it did seem that since listing what I saw as weaknesses was counterproductive, a positive approach made sense. This, by the way, is one way God speaks to us in response to our prayers—guiding us by His Spirit to see a path we hadn't seen before, or giving an understanding, a perception that lines up with who He is.

So I asked God to build character qualities into Dennis's life that I knew would please God. Leadership was first. I had no vision that he'd become the kind of leader he is today; at the time I just knew he was trying to lead me and a tiny little ministry, and yet he still had a lot to learn about being God's man. So I simply began to pray that God would build him into a better leader, *His* kind of leader.

Over the next ten to fifteen years, I continued to pray, not daily, as I had done that first year, but when I did, I asked God to build my husband into the man He created him to be. I considered men in Scripture that I knew had pleased God. For one season I used Daniel as a model, asking God to form in my man the character qualities of integrity, influence, and the refusal to bow to lesser allegiances. In another season I used Joseph as my model, praying that Dennis would develop a similar healthy fear of God, and an ability to see his personal circumstances from God's perspective. They were prayers that would work for any man of God, because they weren't focused on *style*, but rather on *substance*. What qualities can you see in Scripture that you know God would smile over if you prayed them for your husband?

My daughters, prayer is a privilege God gives to involve you in the work He is doing in your husband's life. Prayer is like a little chapel within

Image opposite page: *Rouen Cathedral, West Façade, Sunlight,* oil on canvas, by Claude Monet

the greater church or cathedral you and your husband are building. When you go there, you are seeking to cooperate and partner with God, who has wonderful intentions for your husband, specific "good works" that will last forever. It's like being the foreman on a construction site, misreading the blueprints, reviewing them, and then seeing the Architect's intent at last. Sometimes we misinterpret the plan. Sometimes those we listen to do, too. But the only way to get it right is to repeatedly go back to the biblical blueprints, review how the Architect really wanted to build this marital dwelling of His, and in the chapel of your heart reaffirm your intent to cooperate with His design for you and your husband. When I began praying positively, I started making structural design decisions that lined up with God's purposes and not my own. At last I was cooperating with God's intentions, instead of thinking He got it wrong and I had to set it straight.

My challenge was to love and respect my husband for who he was *at the time*, trusting God would change what needed to be changed in *His* timing. It is the same for me today. Your husband will never become what God has planned if you are more focused on remodeling him than allowing God to do what He does best—building up His son, your husband, to be more and more like Him.

Worth remembering:

- Pray for your man to become more and more like Christ.

- Trust God that He will change what needs to change in His timing.

- Focus on the good you see today.

More stories about my own failures to come! Be kind to yourself in this process, too. We're all learning.

Love you,
Mom

Windows Instead of Walls

Dear Mom,

Okay, so . . . don't let this freak you out. I'm staying. I want this to work. But what do you do when you can't help but think you want out?

Dear daughters,

Somewhere in our second or third year of marriage, I went from a cheerful, confident *I can do this,* to a sobered *This is harder than I thought,* to one day, a desperate *I can't do this! I want to quit.* The thought shook me to the core. I remember feeling trapped and desperate and frightened.

Let me set the stage. . . . We lived in smog-blanketed Southern California—our fourth home in two and a half years—and once again I was in a place with no friends. Not that I would have called anyone. I didn't know how to ask for help. I didn't even know what the problem was. One thing was clear: I needed to get away. Desperate for space, I went into our very tiny master bathroom and locked the door behind me, leaving my husband and baby to fend for themselves. I didn't have any thought for what they might need I was so caught in my own spiral. Maybe it was postpartum depression, which was never diagnosed in those days. All I knew was that I was *done.*

Agitated and panicked, I sat on the edge of the bathtub, then switched to the toilet, then back to the bathtub. My emotions were jumbled. I was annoyed that I was angry and confused, lonely and scared, and I didn't know why. I needed my husband to help me figure it out. But I didn't want to come out and admit I was being childish or silly hiding in the bathroom . . . and wasn't he part of my problem? I was stuck. After an hour or so, the need for something more than porcelain seating and some fresh air drove me to sheepishly unlock the door and return to my world. My husband didn't laugh at me or criticize me or condemn me. I desperately needed his patience and gentleness. We spent lots of time talking that night, working to resolve the issue, whatever it was. And in the end I resolved *I can do this!* once again.

The work of building a cathedral or even a small stone church is difficult. Stone is heavy and has to be carefully cut to stack level and solid. But it's not just walls that have to be built; stonemasons must remember to plan for openings—gothic arches and windows and doorways. Coming out of the bathroom that day and talking was the work of building a doorway between us. Refusing to talk is like building a wall where a lovely opening was meant to be.

That "doorway conversation" (and all those that followed) allowed me to explore my identity as mother and wife and woman over the next two decades, while drawing closer to Dennis as we did this work together. I was learning how to be me, in relation to him. Each conversation was like the work of adding stones to an arched opening. Sometimes the capstone went in and new understanding seemed complete. *Ah, I get it* or *Ah, he gets it! Finally!* Other times it all collapsed in on us and we had to start again. We needed to create those doorways to allow movement into the rooms of each other's lives—so he could understand me, my limits, needs, struggles, fears, hopes, and dreams, and so I could understand his in return. Upward progress was made in all those after-the-kids-were-in-bed conversations, sometimes lasting well past midnight as we often worked on multiple doorways or windows at a time.

Not that I never had thoughts of quitting again. Fast-forward five years, after two more moves and three more kids, all under the age of six. I remember standing in the kitchen of our adorable post-WWII yellow bungalow with six-month-old Rebecca on my hip, the other three in various locations of our 1,800 square feet. And once again I was panicking, thinking, *I can't do this*. This time I didn't want to literally quit, but I felt absolutely confused. Lost. I didn't know who I was anymore. Somewhere in the diapers, Cheerios, toys, and unexpected hurts—both physical and emotional—I felt as if I'd disappeared. *What happened to the old me?* I was the most exhausted thirty-year-old I knew. I wanted to run away . . . just long enough to figure out who I was, and how I was to cope with my life.

It wasn't only daily stresses that made me long for an escape—it was everything coming at us. Over those five years, from San Bernardino to Dallas to Little Rock, we had faced countless sicknesses, a significant financial theft, emergency surgery on our second born, two additional moves, seminary, the sudden death of my husband's father, and most dramatic of all, my near death from an undiagnosed heart defect. We were emotionally exhausted by the pummeling. Through it all, I kept squaring my shoulders, muttering, "I can do this."

But that particular day in my kitchen is still etched

in my mind. I looked up at the wall clock to count the hours till my rescuer would walk in the back door from work. At the exact same moment I thought, *How do I do this mothering routine all day and switch into romantic wife mode after the kids are all in bed? How do I do anything at all when I feel so utterly lost?* I felt completely alone in my quandary. My husband tried to understand and was learning, but I was speaking a female language in which he was not fluent. All the prior dilemmas we had faced, though immensely challenging, somehow seemed surmountable. With the right medical care, the right advisers, the right help, I had believed I could do it, that we could do it together.

But this felt entirely different. Harder than previous moments of crisis because I knew of no expert, no book, no mentor who could diagnose what I was feeling and give a solution.

The irony is that God was totally okay with my saying, "I can't do this." In fact, I think He had been waiting for me to make this discovery for many years. What He wanted was for me to add a short prayer, "But will you show me how?" He wanted me to see that I couldn't do it all, because that was my problem; I felt I "should" be able to do it all, that I was a failure if I couldn't. My circumstances were part of His training process to show me, a firstborn achiever, my need for Him and His strength and His power. Gradually, I realized the ongoing solution was to remain teachable, to never stop being willing to accept what the Master Architect wanted to build in me and in our marriage, and to trust that He was building what I could not.

Over the next two decades I encountered more "I can't do this" situations. . . .

"How can I manage the fear of my child's potentially tragic choice?"

"How can I endure the pain of my prodigal's wanderings?"

"How can I possibly change any more in my marriage?"

"Can I walk the cancer road if that's where I'm headed?"

All of these, and dozens of other "I can't do this" moments that left me feeling totally inadequate, led me to another surrender and then another and another . . . which opened up more windows of light and more

God's ways are mysterious, and our faith develops strong muscles as we negotiate the twists and turns of our lives.

—Elisabeth Elliot

doorways in my marriage and in my relationship with Christ. Through it all I was maturing and becoming more real, more the woman God wanted me to be.

In most cathedrals and even most churches built through the twentieth century, what first catches the eye when entering are the windows—beautiful tall, intricate windows of colored glass through which pours the light of heaven. Jesus, the Light of the World, is love incarnate. And when He met people, what did that light and love do to their souls? The woman at the well felt both fully exposed—"He told me all that I ever did"—and fully loved—"This is indeed the Savior of the world" (John 4:39, 42).

Marriage is to be like our relationship with Jesus: full of exposure for the purpose of healing, as Jesus did for the woman with five husbands, and full of His love because ours is imperfect and weak. Every marriage is rife with impossibilities. But in those times we can experience the wonder of repentance, restoration, and renewal as we risk building doorways to the hidden corners of our souls. Married couples who love genuinely, willingly, and persistently come to see their beloved in a wholly different way because doors and windows have been opened to the interior of their lives that no one else knows.

"I can do all things through him who strengthens me" was Paul's secret for remaining steady in seasons of "plenty and hunger" (Phillipans 4:12–13), when the provision of his next meal seemed impossible, so in my marriage and in my life I have learned He is sufficient when I face another "I can't do this."

These and other trials and mistakes of our early years crumbled our walls of idealism. Through the rubble of these losses we built doorways between one another, and windows to heaven that welcomed more and more of the Light of Christ. What I knew to be true when I said my vows, that building a marriage that pleases God is a lifelong apprentice-ship, would have remained theoretical apart from marital trials and test-ings, which led me "from the realm of reason to the realm of feeling the truth," as Leo Tolstoy put it. God wanted me to cling to Him, to feel His truth, to be intimately acquainted with His power to redeem me and my circumstances for His good. God has taken me from the early years of self-effort, which said, "I can do this," to a deep consciousness today of my inability to do life on my own. And it's a great relief to be at peace with God's design.

When your marriage feels impossible, remember:

- He wants you to experience your own inadequacy.

- It's good to know you can't do it all.

- God will create beautiful windows and doorways for you if you don't quit.

I pray for you that the Spirit will be your closest Companion, that you will learn to hear His whispers to your heart, that you will trust His leading and working more than your own.

Nothing is more important.

Mom

Construction Challenges

Dear Mom,

Things have been good here. I mean really good, for about six months. So much of what you said has helped us, and we've been getting along better. But these last few weeks have been rough. I can't help but think that we're under attack. We're both on edge again, giving in to bickering again, letting things come out of our mouths that really hurt. I keep thinking, Who is he, anyway? *What happened to him, and to me, too?*

Dear daughters,

When we remodeled our house five years ago, we experienced first-hand what any builder has long since learned: The project always takes longer than anticipated, it always costs more than expected, and there are always surprises. Always!

But in building a *marriage* you'll face these three obstacles and more because there is an unseen reality that makes constructing a marriage far more difficult than building a house. The Bible says marriage is a great mystery, which implies there is much we don't know. Though Dennis and I have learned a lot, there is much we still don't understand and probably never will. The marvel of any marriage being a picture of Christ and the church should keep us perpetually in wonder.

I'm sorry things are rough again, that you're seeing flaws too clearly, and that the tools you've been using aren't working right now. I remember nights when your dad and I both went to sleep at night so angry or disappointed or hurt because nothing we had tried made things right.

Has that happened to you? Have you even felt like he's your enemy? The truth is you do sleep with an enemy, though it is not your husband. And to complicate it further, there is more than one enemy in that bed of yours.

Here is what I have learned: I cannot do marriage or life on my own, not just because I'm inadequate but also because I have two unseen enemies. Making it doubly difficult, my husband has two unseen enemies, too. And our marriage is caught in the crossfire. Your marriage is not the problem; your marriage is being targeted!

I battle the enemy of my soul, the father of lies, who is out there always looking for opportunities to accuse me, deceive me, and destroy my faith. And I battle a second foe, my selfishness, which the Bible calls my flesh and which lives within me always demanding to have my way, always finding ways to be right, always justifying my position as best, always elevating myself over others. The Bible calls this sin nature self-righteousness and says my heart is deceitfully wicked. When I first heard this verse in a Bible study, early in our marriage, I thought, *Me? Wicked? I don't think so. Sure, I have a few less-than-perfect qualities, some mistakes in my past, but . . . wicked?* I resisted this unpleasant truth. But like it or not, we are all sin-guilty, so the sooner we quit pretending otherwise the better.

Here is the sad reality: I am thoroughly convinced we have no idea how broken we are, how far we have fallen, and what capacity for relationship was left behind in the garden. Think about it. It's nearly impossible for us to even imagine any relationship not marred by performance, suspicion, or selfishness, right? Even our very best is far less than perfect. The shattered remains of life on planet earth are so normal, so pervasive, we think, *This is all there is. This is all I can hope for.* Like someone born blind or deaf, with no frame of reference for seeing or hearing, so are we in our fallen-ness from what God originally intended.

And if it seems hard to believe me, then listen to brilliant theologian J. I. Packer, who said that even "our best works are shot through with sin and contain something for which we need to be forgiven." Without being born again, we do not have the capacity to imagine a new condition, much less the power to change, nor can we experience what God designed marriage to be: redemptive for me and my husband.

Complicating every marriage is the clash of two sin natures, his and yours, which are joined for life. Not only do I battle the unseen father of lies and my own sinfulness, I am affected by my husband's sinfulness. And he suffers from my failures and flaws. We each have two very different sets of blueprints for building our cathedral, his labeled "My Way" and hers labeled "My Way." Tenaciously we each clutch our own plans, our own ways. No wonder conflict is abundant.

Here is how it works: The sin tendencies of your spouse will eventually be revealed in your marriage. If your spouse has an anger weakness, that will eventually be directed toward you. If the problem is perfectionism, you will feel subjected to those strict standards. If you battle depression or insecurity or inability to trust, your husband will feel the weight of your sorrow, your repeated claims that he really doesn't love you. If one of you has a pattern of manipulation or lying or passivity, it will manifest itself in your marriage. On and on it goes. Our enemy is creative in the ways he intends to snare us, using our natural weaknesses to drag us down to the deeps. This war of the wills and weaknesses in marriage leads to both intended and unintended hurt and pain. It cannot be avoided.

Now for the good news! It can be forgiven and healed. I've learned that the skirmishes in marriage are all about finding who the real enemy is. Husbands and wives mistakenly think it's all her fault or his. And yes, his mistakes and selfishness can cause great pain. Just as your sins hurt him. But the real enemy is not your husband. Selfishness and the evil one are the real enemies of marriage, which is liberating to understand.

"Do you want to get well?" Jesus asked the man lying by the pool. I've always wondered what sort of question that was. Why *wouldn't* he? But perhaps getting well meant no more pity from others or no more free handouts or help. I often wanted to stay just as I was. It was more comfortable to remain in my known condition than to risk learning a new way. When my husband said, "I've always done it this way," about the way he undressed, it sounded selfish to me. But when I was the one who needed to change and responded, "It's who I am; just accept me," it

sounded logical, justifiable.

The fact that Jesus came to heal and restore and make us all well has been changing people and marriages for over two thousand years! He wants to give me something far better than the selfish patterns I cling to—freedom to be all He designed me to be. Yes, my husband needs to recognize his own sinfulness, but I cannot change him. I am only responsible for me. I must choose to surrender, not once but continually, to the only One who has the power to defeat these foes. It's a two-step adjustment. Step one is recognizing and admitting my selfishness, my sin, and step two is saying no to its strong pull to get even, to fire back, to be right, to prove him wrong, or to retreat into my shell of self-protection. Confess your own selfishness and say yes to giving grace, giving a blessing, or saying nothing. Surrendering to His way is never easy, but it is always right and always brings peace.

When we say, "Not my will, but thy will, O God," another victory is won, and the father of lies has lost another attempt to help you close up those doorways and windows

Photo above: Saint-Chappelle, Paris

with rock. And each triumph allows God to set in place a beautiful piece of glass in the cathedral of your marriage through which He wants to shine His light. *Miraculous* is the only word to describe making a shattered heart a thing of clear beauty once again.

Here's a dilemma some of your friends may be facing—when a Christian is married to a non-Christian. They will still have the same challenges you do with sin patterns and selfishness, but if one spouse does not have the power of Christ to make life change, there is an added burden. I have heard hundreds of stories of how God redeemed marriages like this. Two couples I know very well started out unequally yoked, and God worked in their lives in very different ways. No two are the same—a specialty of God, which I love. A verse that works for any wife says, "They may be won without a word by the conduct of their wives, when they see your respectful and pure conduct" (1 Peter 3:1–2).

Any husband can go through a time when he's not living the way Christ would desire, and the surest way to *change* that man is not to tell him what he needs to do, but to continue to love and respect him and pray for him. An old saying fits here: "I'd rather see a sermon lived than hear one." Modeling godly behavior and attitudes is far better than preaching it to him! I hope you can encourage your friends in this situation to believe God and not quit on their men, because the God who raises the dead can do the same with a spiritually dead husband! Another amazing mystery.

Your dad and I now engage in far fewer battles. No more trying to impress or compete or win. The safety and peace we feel with each other is what we both always wanted, but we didn't understand at the beginning how long it took to get there. Yes, we still disagree, and yes, we still hurt each other, but we are so much quicker to forgive and move on. We understand we have a common enemy, and it is not each other.

And we laugh a lot. We laugh at our weaknesses, our quirkiness, our inability to communicate—still, because we know we are forgiven. Teasing each other can now be done without feeling accused or condemned. All that is gone, and it is delightful. So know that it might be hard for a while, but after years of practice, it does get easier. I promise.

We have talked many times about what each would do if God takes one of us home before the other. I have said repeatedly that I have no intention of getting married again, because I don't want to learn to live with another sin nature all over again! The two enemies I now know are enough for one lifetime!

So remember this:

- Your husband is not your enemy, nor is he "the problem."

- Be honest about your selfishness with each other. It's worth the risk.

- Confess your sin every time and grant forgiveness freely. It keeps the windows clean and clear.

- You are only responsible for you. Let God do the work in your husband's heart. He's the expert, not you.

May the glimmer of your marriage invite others to want to know the One who gives you life,

Mom

THE ONE INTERIOR DESIGNER

Finishing Touches

Now that we've traveled forty years of marriage by faith, I have come to realize the Holy Spirit is my dearest Friend. Misunderstood, neglected, and ignored, this greatest Gift to those of us who believe is the One who has most helped me become who I am today. He has whispered truth, guided me to the best paths, and given me wisdom when I asked. He has gently nudged me to speak . . . and at other times He has nudged me to

Marriage is not a DIY project. It only works well when I follow the Architect and Interior Designer's directions each and every day.

be silent. When I've listened to His leading, I've never been sorry. When I haven't listened, I've had regrets.

Following Him has been slow and arduous, not because He is not a good leader, but because I haven't always been a willing follower. Whispers require attentiveness. And understanding means learning His language. Being conversant is necessary to develop friendship with this Master Interior Designer. Guess I'm a slow learner, because it's taken years. If you're not there yet, be patient with yourself. Jesus said, "My sheep hear my voice" (John 10:27). You will in time, too.

If you had asked me in year two or four or six of our marriage if I was trusting God in my life and marriage, I would have answered yes. If you'd asked if I was walking in the Spirit, that, too, would have received an affirmative. And it would have been true. In that time, in that place, I was trusting Him as much as I knew how. But from His perspective He knew I had a long way to go. Because He loves me and wants me to know Him—still *so* much more than I pursue Him on any given day—He is going to continue to show me how I need Him, so I can then experience His strength and redemption at work.

Have you ever painted a room and then stood back and

decided it was three shades too close to hideous? Have you brought home a piece of furniture and realized it was all wrong for the room? Just as a skilled interior designer can save us from DIY obsession, so, too, can God help us avoid costly mistakes . . . or heal them. In every marriage, God is constantly, gently exposing places of brokenness, hoping we will call upon Him and invite Him in to heal us. Books and counselors and friends are helpful, too, but they're most helpful if they encourage us to put our hand in His. He has promised to never leave or forsake me. He is always present. And that was and is the ultimate lesson in marriage: to learn that marriage is not a DIY project. It only works well when I follow the Architect and Interior Designer's directions each and every day.

One of my favorite books is *The Valley of Vision*. Beautifully written prayers from the Puritan tradition, different from our own spontaneous style today, have inspired and tugged my heart to a more truth-filled, more sacred approach to the Trinity. These words, adapted from three of my favorite prayers in the book, summarize the life lessons I've attempted to paint for you in these last letters.

O God, the Holy Spirit,
that which I know not,
teach thou me. . . .
Let me never lose sight of my need of a Savior,
or forget that apart from Him I am nothing,
and can do nothing. . . .

I thank you that you have made me capable of knowing you,
the Author of all being . . .
of enjoying you,
the source of all happiness. . . .

It is an amazing thing to see deity in a creature,
speaking, acting, filling, shining through it.
That nothing is good but you,
that I am near good when I am near you.
That to be like you is a glorious thing.

—from *The Valley of Vision*

Remember that God is working good into your life through each battle you face beside your husband. He who began a good work is faithful to complete it. He will not stop the purifying of your souls, the transforming work of shining His light on the broken fragments of your hearts.

The world watches. Be aware that you are observed—by your children, your friends, and others you don't even know. The cathedral that you are building with your husband is meant to reflect the image of God through your lives and your union. Look to Him, again and again, on how to do that.

Love,
Mom

CHAPTER 4

While I love music, I am very much a consumer, not a creator. But my lack of ability didn't stop me from trying to coax any fragment of musical potential out of my children. My attempts to make us a musical family started with Ashley and Samuel taking piano lessons for several years. Then I had this genius idea that Ashley could teach her three younger sisters basic piano. And it worked! We even had a mini-recital. Ashley was amazing with her siblings. I should have named her Grace, for she was an incredibly patient teacher with her little sisters. But after one year, I gave up, realizing that musical genes just didn't reside in the Raineys.

Even though music isn't my forte, I know enough to understand it has many parallels to marriage. Every piece of music begins with the same foundational elements: a single staff of five lines and four spaces; and the beginning notes, do, re, mi, fa, sol, la, ti—seven distinct sounds. Beginning with those simple symbols, hundreds of thousands of masterpieces have been written over the centuries.

In the beginning, before everything was broken forever, the foundational marriage tools for Adam and Eve were as basic—and potent—as these elementary tools of music. God first formed man, put him in a place named Eden (like the boundaries of five lines and four spaces), with instructions to work and keep the garden and not to eat the forbidden fruit. Then He created a helper for Adam, Eve, and concluded this pinnacle of creation with what we know as a marriage pronouncement for everyone who would follow—to leave father and mother and become one flesh. At that moment, marriage was established and simply defined. Though we would love to know more details of this creation performance—which was celebrated by an audience of watching angels who sang for joy—looking at the raw simplicity of the very first couple's beginning gives us needed perspective now. Before any mistakes were made by either partner, Eve's foundational purpose with Adam was described as *helper*. Profound with potential, yet simple in design.

Though much changed after the fall, God's intentions for me as a wife did not. Eve was made to be helper, and so am I. Playing this song in harmony with my husband hasn't been easy or without lots and lots of mistakes, but hard doesn't mean it's wrong. It is still the original score.

ALLOWING HIM TO TAKE THE LEAD
The Maestro's Handwritten Score

So, Mom,

> *You're good at letting Dad take the lead and being the helper. But I'm not. I feel like I know better than he does. How come he gets to*

be the deciding factor? Sometimes I think the whole "man as leader"
dealio is more than a tad old-fashioned. Women today are working as
hard as men are, competing in the marketplace, contributing, just as
they are. But we're supposed to come home and be the "little woman"?

Dearest daughters,

Okay, prepare for a blunt answer to such a blunt question! To add a little perspective, women have worked as hard as men since time began—unless they were born into the nobility at Downton Abbey! Your great-grandmother worked very hard on the farm with conditions that would make all of us wilt—no air conditioning or central heat or appliances, for starters. She grew and canned all their food, made almost all their clothing, served a very bitter father-in-law who lived with them, and took in ironing to help make ends meet. So keep in mind that your generation of career-minded women isn't the first to seek balance in work and marriage.

As to why he "gets" to be the leader . . . I'll get there. It'll take a while, so be patient while I tell you how I came to understand this challenging concept.

When I got married, I was eager to begin making beautiful music in my marriage. I wanted to play my part well to harmonize with him. I knew "helper" was the title on my sheet of music, but what did that mean practically? Other than cooking and doing our laundry, I couldn't think of many truly helpful tasks, which for me, a task-oriented woman, was my initial approach. Honestly, I had no idea what the helper concept really meant.

The only way to figure it out is to go back to the original score in Genesis. I remember learning the puzzling fact that our perfect God made Adam incomplete: a stunning enigma! Which reminds me of a story I recently read about a Beethoven manuscript discovered hidden away in a library. What was odd to the musicians who began to play it was a long section, badly faded, that appeared to be nothing but rests. Eventually they realized the newly discovered piece was but part of a larger work. It was incomplete alone. They could only wonder what genius and beauty they were missing by having only a partial score. If the other parts could be found, the one they possessed would make complete sense.

And so is the mystery of marriage. Both parts of the original score are needed for what God intended to say. *Mystery* is a word to describe something unfathomable, something we humans can't understand. God is a mystery, Jesus is a mystery, the gift of salvation is a mystery, and the Bible even calls marriage a mystery. Complicating it further, the Bible says marriage is a picture of Christ with His church, which is pictured as a bride. Somehow in some enigmatic way, my marriage (and yours) is a picture of God Himself. It is an echo of a piece of supremely beautiful music that once was heard on earth before the fall. I don't understand the mystery of His music, but I believe it is true. By faith.

Returning to the story, Eve was *fashioned*, a word that speaks to the beautiful, not made out of dirt like the man. Importantly, God didn't create her to fix a mistake, for Adam's incomplete state was intentional. She, too, was made with intentionality to complete Adam. A perfectly matched pair. Two halves that fit like two puzzle pieces to make one whole song. Together they would reflect the image of God. Together they would rule the earth and reproduce godly children who would repeat the cycle: reflect, reign, and reproduce in every generation.

A duet. Two complementary voices made to harmonize. As co-regents, Adam and Eve were complete without any dissonance. Together their maleness and femaleness produced a harmony of beauty much like the rising and falling of notes on a sheet of music. The addition of her life to his elevated and enhanced his manhood. Without her he had been less. He was wowed by her beauty, her entirely different capacities, and the energy her presence provided. He eagerly elevated her female glory and included her in everything he did. (We do not know how long they lived in this perfectly harmonious relationship before the fateful fall, but might it have been a long time?) Their completeness mirrored the image of the relationship in the Trinity itself.

So how do our marriages do the same today? And why is your husband

The addition of
Eve's life to Adam's
elevated
and
enhanced
his manhood.
Without her, he had been less.

the leader? Like it or not, because God made him, designed him, coded his DNA to lead. This does not mean you cannot lead at all or ever. Your original design as a woman was to be a co-regent in Eden, remember? You have leadership skills, and so do I. But in our marriage, while I lead in a variety of ways, I choose to look to him as my leader, willingly accepting this created order as part of the mystery God has written. I admit I don't always like it, nor do I understand it, but by following the music together we've found harmony.

Keeping with our sheet music imagery, my husband's design to lead was not his choice. There is a Conductor of this duet of ours, and it is not my husband. He has his part to play that requires him to pay close attention to the Conductor, who directs both of us in our marriage. Every musician must watch and follow closely the notations in the music and the direction of the conductor, or the piece will not delight as it was intended to do. Each instrument in any particular composition is important to the whole even if during portions of the piece the violins are more prominent than the oboes, or the kettledrums more than the clarinets.

I will say more about the leading part of the duet in future letters, because marriage is much more complicated than a simple melody like "Mary Had a Little Lamb," played with one hand on four notes in C major. It's too much for one letter.

One very important last thought. I've discovered an interesting parallel with music and marriage. Every piece of music is notated with precision, yet there are still decisions to be made when it is performed. Free improvisation is a musical term which means a musician will spontaneously create something new within the framework of the piece as he is performing. Like improvising a recipe by adding a new ingredient that gives a new twist to an old favorite, or an actor passionately improvising as he adds to his memorized lines, I believe God gives us great freedom to create in our marriages within the basic structure and form He designed.

Viewing marriage as an exquisite piece of music, as multifaceted as a symphony, elevates your vision for the elegance and beauty God originally intended. Both of you have to decide if you will follow the Conductor's leading or go your own way. Long ago I decided I would follow God's design even when it made no sense. Today it feels right that both of us are becoming our best. Together we are both more productive, more creative, and more complete than we would have been alone.

So here are two musical tips:

- Don't rewrite God's music, but play it with gusto and all the creativity you have!

- Always watch and follow the Conductor's lead. He knows what He's doing.

I don't want to miss one note of the symphony God wants to write with us, and I hope you want the same in your marriage, too. God will make beautiful music with your union if you do.

Much love always,
Mom

FINDING CALM IN THE STORM
Esther's Song

Dear Mom,

You've always been such a good helper for Dad, and I know he's always appreciated that in you. But I'm finding that when I try to help the Hubs, all I get is pushback. What am I doing wrong?

Dear girls,

Thank you for noticing that, though please know it hasn't always been so easy. What you saw and what happened behind the scenes weren't always the same. I hope reviewing the original score for Adam and Eve reminded you of the big picture. Another story might help in a more practical way.

One winter evening early in our marriage, we went to a church where my new husband had been asked to speak. I remember sitting near the front, feeling proud of him, because I genuinely thought he did a great job. But I also noticed a few mistakes, mostly grammatical errors that I'd never noticed in everyday conversation. On the drive home he asked what I thought about his speaking, and I told him I was impressed, that I felt he communicated clearly and effectively. Then it was quiet for a few minutes as we continued driving home. In the silence I rehearsed what I wanted to say, took a deep breath, and said, "Do you mind if I mention something I think you could correct?"

He said he'd be grateful if I did. I was immensely relieved. I had taken a risk with my young husband and had no idea if he would feel attacked or put down. My motive was to help him improve. I wanted to be his ally, his helper in a practical sense. By asking permission to be heard, he understood my motives and intentions were for his good.

Each of you has strengths your husband doesn't have. He needs what you bring to the relationship, but the key is in how you use your strengths to help. It takes a bit of wisdom and skill to help in a harmonious, nonthreatening way. Don't bail on trying to figure it out if you run into some trouble up front.

I know you all remember the story of Esther. One of our favorite bedtime storybooks was a beautifully illustrated version about this orphan girl who won a beauty pageant and became queen of Persia. This woman, who lived millennia ago, married a man who did not know her God, which makes her story even more instructive. Esther lived out Paul's later instruction to wives to "be submissive to your own husbands so that even if any of them are disobedient to the word, they may be won without a word by the behavior of their wives" (1 Peter 3:1 NASB). Queen Esther's wise behavior prevented a holocaust. The way she humbly and creatively dealt with an impossible situation gave me encouragement in many hard circumstances of my own. She is a mentor for every wife.

Even though Esther's wedding was undoubtedly as spectacular as those of modern royals, she found herself in a marital crisis sooner than she'd ever imagined. Her husband, the king, had some cabinet members who manipulated him with very bad advice, and unbeknownst to him, the result was going to send Esther to her death, along with every other Jewish person in Persia, which ruled the world. Just this piece of the story is a reminder that our husbands can also make decisions that bring us wives unintentional harm. No man, even a king who has abundant resources and advisers, will avoid making some bad decisions. Marriage is risky business. But God delivered Esther, and He can deliver us today, too.

The crescendo of the story is Esther's response. Upon the wise and godly advice of her cousin, who adopted her and raised her, Esther began praying. She also fasted and called on her friends to join with her. The situation was a life-and-death crisis, and it demanded an equally dramatic and serious approach.

When I think about what Esther must have felt, considering her imminent death along with the entire Jewish race, I'm amazed that she did not panic and dash off to the throne room crying and screaming. Many of us wives, had we been in her shoes, would have panicked and with a raised, high-pitched voice screamed, "How could you have done this! What stupidity! Do you not see what is about to happen because of your edict?" Don't most of us feel like doing that when our husbands make decisions that hurt us? When your dad announces to me that he just booked another trip that I must attend only because I'm "the wife," I have felt angry, not valued, as though his agenda is always more important than mine. Being flexible (for this nonspontaneous, routine-oriented homebody) and willing to travel *just because he needs me* has been one of the unanticipated trials in my marriage. I have not always handled this well, and Dennis would heartily agree. Every wife knows those flash points in her marriage where her husband has created a situation that feels like a crisis or is in fact a stressful circumstance, whether it is intentional or unintentional. It could be a small thing that feels huge, like perpetual tardiness, or a truly big thing, like perpetually not paying bills on time, leading to the electricity being cut off. Every marriage struggle is unique, even though the struggle of responding well is common to all wives. Only recently have I practiced believing the best and not reacting in this oft-repeated travel crisis of ours.

Esther was far wiser than I. Instead of overreacting, she invited her husband to a very nice dinner she'd prepared . . . wait for it . . . after three days! (Have I ever waited three days before telling your dad I disagree with a decision he's made? I don't think so.) On the following day, again over food (don't we all feel more ready to tackle hard stuff when we've been well fed?), she asked permission to inform the king that he had made a big mistake. She was asking to correct him. Let's be clear: It was very risky to challenge the king of Persia. As in, he could've immediately had her beheaded. But her cautious and calm attitude and actions demonstrated to her husband that she was not a threat, she was not against him; instead, she honored him. She showed wisdom and a heart that trusted God's sovereignty over all. Famously, now she is remembered for having said, "If I perish, I perish."

When Esther asked her husband for the privilege of being heard, she communicated respect for him as a man and as a leader. I learned that myself in that first year of marriage when I asked my husband if I could offer corrections that would help him be a better communicator. He felt my respect, from all the kudos I gave him for the great job he did. He saw my offer to help as an asset, not a condemnation. Again, the heart of the matter was, and still is, my *attitude*. He will know if you are for him or if you are against him in how you approach him. And it has to be real, dear daughters, not an act. It has to be something we've gotten straight in our own hearts.

An oft-repeated criticism from judges on the popular TV singing competitions is, "You need to put more of your heart into this song. I want to sense that you feel it when you sing." And so with my husband, my attitude can say what my words do not. I may be careful to say the right words, but if my heart is not in it, the result is hollow and he will know it. Our men are not stupid. We may think we have more sensitivity, more intuition, more emotional depth, but any husband can sense when his wife's heart is against him. Esther got hers in the right place by calming her fears, controlling her anger, and trusting God to work before her, beside her, and even through her. In fact, God woke the king in the night and prepared him for what Esther was about to reveal. She could not see how God was working behind the scenes, but she prayed, believed, and moved when the time was right.

How did she know the time was right? My guess is she didn't. Perhaps her request for a second banquet was stalling on her part. But here is where we women must walk closely with the Spirit, who I believe was working in Esther's heart, leading her each step of the way. He makes no mistakes, and when we walk with Him, we can be sure our steps will be just as sure as were hers.

Remember in the crises that will come:

- Don't panic or overreact.

- Ask, "Can I talk to you about something?" before bringing something difficult or potentially threatening to him.

- Pray for wisdom to speak in words he can hear and absorb.

May you each be like my friend Esther, with hearts that trust the sovereignty of God and not the fears that threaten to overwhelm. It will be music to your husband's ears.

With love,
Mom

Finding the Best Instructor

Dear Mom,

The Hubs simply has to grow up. I have enough to deal with in raising the kids. How come you never told me I had to raise a husband, too? I swear he'd walk out the door without socks if I couldn't find the pair he was looking for. He'd forget to pick up the kids at practice if I didn't call him every day at 4:45. And how did it become my job to schedule every "playdate" he wants to have? He has a cell, too! It's like he doesn't see that I'm stretched to my breaking point. Help!

Okay, my daughters,

If this is really true of your man—and I know it's not out of the realm of possibility for some men to want their wives to take care of things their mothers used to do—my guess is it's not a genuine crisis but just a habit that irritates you. I will say that most husbands do need some training from their wives in learning about women in general and you in particular, but tracking a to-do list for him does not have to be your job. That's up to you. So what if he goes to work without socks? Might be a good thing. This letter is about our female tendency toward high control, but first another story about how I chose poorly.

Your Gramma Rainey called her son the road runner. I should have realized it wasn't just an affectionate name, but true to his nature. When I was a kid, my dad rarely traveled for business, and our only family vacation was our annual migration south to visit family. Now I was living with a man always on the go for his job . . . *and* his free time.

Before the days of cell phones, your dad would maximize his time by using airport pay phones while we were waiting to make connections. And I'd sit and wait and watch as every last passenger boarded the plane while he continued to chat on the phone, seemingly oblivious to the time and the imminent departure of the plane. As my nervousness grew, I'd get up and go remind him of the time, sometimes more than once, or I'd get angry that I was having to wait and that *he* might cause *me* to be inconvenienced by missing our flight! The nerve! I began to think of him as incompetent. I wondered how he ever made it onto a plane without me.

In spite of my valiant efforts to revise his plane-boarding routine, he never changed. Finally, after years of travel anxiety, I gave up and focused on the fact that he was a grown man, wearing a watch on his wrist. I decided that if we missed a flight, which we never did, it would be his responsibility to rebook connections and deal with all the ramifications. I chose to trust him. My great surprise was that giving up trying to change him and choosing to trust allowed me to relax and not stress.

Travel trials are not what you're dealing with, but I bet it's more than finding his socks. Whether he's carrying his fair share, how much guy time he seems to need, his volatility, or his lack of leadership at home are just a few of the common issues wives face that may show up in your house, too. Trusting God to work is a delicate balance of waiting and praying. The travel issue was really my problem, not his. And that is the first place to start when you feel like he has got to change—look first to find your part in the situation, whatever it is.

You see, I was feeling responsible for something that was NOT my responsibility. If he had needed my help, he would have asked (or could have asked). Or if we routinely missed flights, I could have respectfully approached the issue. The fact was, I felt he needed my help when he did not. And moreover, I wasn't trusting him. I felt I had to pester him if I was to get to where we were going. It was particularly hard when we were heading home, where I most long to be.

The same is true with a husband who isn't leading. How much of it is your expectation of what a husband should do? Are you being impatient and he knows it? Maybe he is afraid to try because he is sure you will be disappointed. If you relax and trust patiently, maybe he will realize he needs to step up.

What I was dealing with in airports for so many years (did you catch the plural *years*?) was the perpetual struggle of how to be a helper without feeling critical and then becoming nagging. Helping is not instructing. It is not mothering. It is not enabling.

The question is, does your husband want and need your help or not? It is yours to find out if he does and what kind of help would be beneficial to him. There will be seasons in his life when he's not open to your help.

Helping is not instructing. It is not mothering. It is not enabling.

If this is one of those, then let it be and trust the Conductor of your marriage to set him right. Your husband will not play his part like a seasoned master when he's just learning. Give him grace and time.

Here is what happens with many of us wives: Once children arrive in a marriage, the lines often blur between being a mom and being a wife. As a mother, I am constantly helping my children learn skills needed for life, like tying shoes, eating neatly, making beds, doing homework, and a million other tasks on their way to adulthood. I am the teacher, my child the learner. I am the mentor, my child the disciple. Mothers are constantly giving commands, directions, and instructions, all for the purpose of raising responsible, mature children equipped for adulthood. It's hard to switch out of that mode when the hubby comes in and leaves the door open, just like the kids, or can't find something and asks where it is, just like the kids, or gets angry over something you think is silly, just like the kids. I know! It takes discipline and self-control not to view him as a kid, too.

But with my husband, God does not want me to give an authoritative kind of help. Instructing him on how to perform his part of the music is *not* my job. I don't "instruct him" about what to wear or how to eat his food or where to put his shoes or tools or newspapers. Or I shouldn't. While I was the authority with you, my children, I am not with my husband. He is my partner, my equal, not my protégé or student. I'm not his teacher (which doesn't mean I can't teach him things). Your dad doesn't like being bossed or corrected any more than I do when he becomes parental with me.

Recently we finished remodeling the living room, and I was a tad protective of our newly reupholstered couch and newly cleaned rugs. Dennis likes to eat in the living room, especially on weekends, and when he began choosing the couch, I said, after realizing this was becoming his new favorite spot, "Would you mind not eating here, but instead sit on that chair?"

He pushed back, saying, "But I want to eat here."

Let God be your husband's music instructor. He wrote the man's part and knows how it should be played.

I explained, with a degree of kindness, that eating on the leather chair would be better because it wouldn't stain as easily, and the darker rug under the chair wouldn't show spots. I gave him an alternative. I wasn't being bossy, this time, and he understood the logic after I explained the benefit of keeping the rug clean and preserving the couch. (Saving money speaks to him!) We reached an acceptable compromise: He could eat in comfort and watch TV, and I could keep the newly recovered couch and rug beneath it spot-free. I expressed my desire and my reasons, knowing it is our house, not my house. We wives can feel possessive of our homes, deciding he can have this one room or that one corner for his gear. Maybe we have a control issue? Do you think?

Maybe you have people who report to you at work, and your instinct is to come home and relate to your husband as you do your employees, though I would hope your employees don't feel bossed around by you. Regardless, we women can come across as high-powered and corrective with our husbands. And that is not what God had in mind. It's not the kind of togetherness we married for.

Remember, helping is more of an attitude than an action:

- Are you treating him as your friend and the love of your life?

- Are your words and tone of voice more like his instructor or boss?

- If you need something specific, let him know gently. But don't obsess over things that really don't matter. Life is short.

- Let God be your husband's music instructor. He wrote the man's part and knows how it should be played.

Hugs,
Mom

> Traditionally we are taught, and instinctively we long, to give where it is needed—and immediately. Eternally, woman spills herself away in driblets to the thirsty, seldom being allowed the time, the quiet, the peace, to let the pitcher fill up to the brim.
>
> —Anne Morrow Lindbergh,
> *Gift From the Sea*

Listen to the Repeated Refrain

Dear Mom,

I get it: Ask permission on big or threatening issues and don't be his mother or teacher. I'm still digesting that. . . . But there has to be more to this helper thing for my everyday life. A deeper part of it. How do I find satisfaction and meaning in that role?

Dear daughters,

There is something mystical and veiled yet very significant wrapped up in the word *helper* that we will never grasp completely. I say that because I want you to know that being confused is normal. At the same time, I want you to see that being a wife is of great importance. It is a profound and eternally meaningful assignment. In the day-to-day of ordinary life we easily lose sight of the honor, high calling, and even nobility we felt on our wedding day. Yes, there are practical ways to wisely help that I've written about, but there are also hidden soul works that God wants to do in your husband's life with your help.

Over the last few years as I've created and written the books for the Adorenaments line of Christmas ornaments, each with a unique name of Christ, I've grown in my appreciation and wonder for the depth of meaning in each of Jesus' names. And not only that, but the act of naming is a divine work that began in eternity past, continued in creation, and has been bestowed on us, His creations, as we name our children, give endearing names to our spouses, speak words that give life or death (more on this in another letter), and influence on a global scale the evolution of language itself. If we remember that it is God Himself, the Author of life, who gave names to define and explain marriage, it will help us to revere His word choices instead of revile them. No decision of God's is ever made on a whim, nor are His actions anything but deliberate, precise, and deep with layered meanings we will not see or appreciate until heaven. So as we talk about our name as wives, *helper*, ask Him to take away any anxiety or fear or anger you might feel toward the term. Remember, God does not stutter or misspeak. Ever.

In the early days of our marriage I remember learning that the Holy Spirit is named Helper, and making the connection that my title of helper can't be second-class if He Himself has the same title. But it wasn't until several years ago that I went past that to identify what the Holy Spirit does for me that I could actually imitate as a wife. Sometimes I am surprised at how slow I am. Seriously. So I actually looked at what the Bible said about the Holy Spirit as my Helper, and it was a rich discovery. This is serious theology, daughters of mine, but I know you can handle it. Besides, I'm a strong believer in women becoming theologians. It's good for your brains! And your faith.

Before Jesus went to the cross, He told His followers that He would send them a Helper, that He would not leave them alone as orphans. (I've always liked that part. Who would ever wish to be orphaned and alone?) Then Jesus explained what the Holy Spirit will do for us when He comes to live within: "He will be with you forever" (see John 14:16). The culminating promise of every wedding ceremony is "till death do us part," which is very much like what Jesus promised. Both bride and groom repeat this vow because both need that security. But in the day-to-day of real married life, does he know you are "with him forever"?

An inseparable bond is the bedrock of any great marriage. Your dad and I have restated our vows a thousand times over the years—not formally, as you might picture it, or romantically, though we've said those words to each other over dinner and candles—but rather in the normal ebb and flow of life. We've said, "I'd marry you all over again," or "I'm so glad I've got you, that I'm not doing life alone." It's kind of like the theme music in a great movie, played at all the pivotal parts, with reprises that are both big and epic as well as quiet and ethereal—a whispered refrain.

Commit to humming that music in your husband's ear. To reinforcing your dedication and love. And it's not just stating the positive, but also refusing to voice the negative threats of leaving or of divorce. Your husband needs both your repeated commitment and your verbal restraint when hope feels lost.

When Jesus said the Holy Spirit would be "with you forever," He meant the Holy Spirit is *present* with me today. Now. Presence matters. When we were raising you kids, I wanted and needed your dad's presence

with me in the daily work of parenting. Daily presence says "I'm with you" when he changes diapers, helps with work around the house, shares in correction and training, and truly remains my partner in this all-important parenting job we have chosen to do together. And he needs my presence with him. If he could have had his wish, your dad would have asked me to accompany him on every single trip he has ever taken. But he learned in an understanding way that I simply couldn't live at his pace, so we found a compromise. But we've been over that!

And here I will brag on Ashley, who when Michael was in residency, would often load up the boys in their car seats and drive to the hospital to have dinner with him when he was on call, just so they could be together. Sometimes she took a pot of chili and they shared their dinner with other staff members; other times she just drove through McDonald's. But the important part was this—she sacrificed what would have been easiest for her in order to be with him. Her motives were to be with him in what he was doing, his life's calling, and to get to know those he worked with. And she said, "I wanted them to see and know Michael had a wife." Her actions were proactive and intentional toward protecting her marriage.

We marry to be with each other for life, but after the "I do," it's far too easy to drift into separate, independent living. Being a helper to your husband means being committed to him for life and being present in his life as his partner. Presence matters. It feeds his soul. By contrast, absence has consequences. Remember how Adam and Eve hid from the presence of God? Be present with your husband, not isolated. But there's more to the Spirit's soundtrack for our marriage.

Trust is supremely important in family relationships, especially marriage, and trust is built on truth telling. God is the source of all truth, and Jesus said the Helper is "the Spirit of truth." Black-and-white rules would be much simpler for me: Always speak the truth no matter when or where. Got it. But helping my husband means "speaking the truth *in love*," which of course the Holy Spirit is perfectly able to do because He is God and He is Love. I am neither. But it must be my goal. And my great hope and confidence is that the eternal Helper will give me aid.

Listen to the Spirit, whose words of truth are music to you, whose gentle guiding is the beat, the rhythm of the heavenly soundtrack of His glorious purposes.

Here is the difficulty. The notion that a wife must say everything she thinks to her husband with no sense of discernment or respect or restraint is as flawed as outright lies. We wives don't always need to say everything we think and feel. We can and must speak truth, *but* carefully choose the most accurate words. Without exaggeration! In addition, *all* truth doesn't need to be spoken *all* at once. The Holy Spirit lovingly tells me one truth at a time. Thankfully, He doesn't reveal how flawed I am all at once. Likewise, I am learning to choose what to say and when and how, "according to the need of the moment," so my words "give grace to those [my husband especially] who hear" (Ephesians 4:29 NASB).

The Holy Spirit never exaggerates the truth, thankfully, but He also never tempts us to sin. As it says in James 1:13, "He himself tempts no one." If your husband is given to outbursts of anger, then you must wisely limit the kind of information that might enflame him and tempt him to sin. Or if your husband is jealous of your close relationship with your sister, you might make the choice to minimize how much you talk about her until he grows to understand she is not more important to you than he is. Sometimes when Dennis and I are watching TV, I'll remind him not to watch a commercial that is provocative. I'll either say, "I'd prefer you not watch that," or I'll ask him an unrelated question to divert his attention. I'm not nagging, and he knows my desire is to help. Often he's just sitting there with flat brain waves after a hard day at work. His defenses are down, and he understands my motives. I'm not trying to control, but to help, gently, speaking the truth in love.

Listen to the Spirit, whose words of truth are music to you, whose gentle guiding is the beat, the rhythm of the heavenly soundtrack of His glorious purposes. Pay attention when He pauses for the notated rests in the music. Don't run ahead and insert your opinions and emotions, thereby getting in the way of what God might want to do. Give your husband space to hear the voice of the Spirit speaking, too, just as Elijah did when he heard the sound of a gentle, blowing wind. Imitate Him, don't try to be Him. The Holy Spirit is a *gentle* Counselor to us, and so should we be with our husbands.

And just this week I've been thinking how remark-able this statement is: "He will not speak on his own authority, but whatever he hears he will speak," and "He will glorify me [Jesus]" (John 16:13–14). Those statements startled me when I read them, thinking about what I do as a wife. How often do I make sure I am not speaking on my own authority? How often do I pause to ask God what He wants me to say to my husband rather than what my sinful flesh wants to say? Does all that I say glorify Jesus? I'm afraid I prattle on far too often without listening first to the Spirit.

Just as we who know Christ as Savior long for heaven one day, so, too, we in Christian marriages long for a heavenly marriage, one that echoes what the Creator of all made us to know and experience. Though a perfect marriage is not possible, we can hope to grow a more lovely one by focusing on the holy. Find your guide for how to make your marriage work in Scripture, and in older, more mature godly women. Set your sights on God's standards, on His excellent dreams for your marriage, and don't go for advice to those who aren't biblically strong. Mediocrity or worse will be the result if you do.

There are many other verses that describe the Holy Spirit, which you will discover yourselves in the years to come. Ask the Spirit of truth to reveal more of Himself and heaven's authenticity to you. He wants to do that for you, and it's better hearing it from Him than from me anyway.

Remember as you train your ears to hear His soundtrack:

- Your husband will always need to hear both verbal

and nonverbal reminders that say, "I'm with you forever."

- Presence matters.

- Speak truth with love and restraint.

Yours for a new generation of wives, worth more than rubies,
Mom

TRUSTING THE CONDUCTOR

A Peaceful Duet

If I were a musician, I would compose a hymn or song that centers your heart on the noble and supremely valuable calling of helper because too many days it feels far from noble and holy. Something with a catchy tune to stick in your brain and keep you focused on eternal truth, not distracted by the emotional declarations and debates of today that claim new truth, new understanding of God's words about men and women in marriage.

An old hymn says "Trust and obey, for there's no other way to be happy in Jesus, but to trust and obey." Like you, I still don't understand why God arranged the notes in us as He did, but within that arrangement are limitations. Life is full of limitations, like the gravity that secures our home and possessions safely to the ground but keeps us from flying like the birds. There are countless more. Wisdom accepts them in humility without finding fault with God and trusts His hand to make something beautiful with what He has given.

Today couples underestimate the difficulty in a lifetime marriage commitment. Even more, they vastly underestimate the power of God to rescue and redeem and restore. Mistakes can't be avoided. Grief will visit all. But none of the hard days or hard seasons negate the greater power of God to work miracles in your life and your marriage.

Though Dennis and I have not arrived at some unattainable place of perfection, we have arrived at a place of greater fulfillment and satisfaction in our marriage than I ever thought possible. It's a great relief to finally know that I am not responsible for my husband. It is not my job to name his weaknesses or sins for him. It is not my job to meet all his needs, either. I am responsible for explaining how his actions affect me or hurt me. It is another way I help him so that he can do what he's been charged to do—which is to "live with your wives in an understanding way" (1 Peter 3:7). Finally, it is liberating to trust God with all of who my husband is, all of his days, and for the length of his life. His life is in the Conductor's hands, and that's how I want it.

As you face repeated crises of faith regarding the way God created both of you and the notes he gave you to play in your marriage piece, remember God is the Conductor of your symphony. He formed man first, and fashioned the

woman second for purposes greater than we can understand, to speak to the watching and listening universe a message, a song, a wonder. It is a fact. Don't be one to whom God says, "Will the faultfinder contend with the Almighty?" (Job 40:2 NASB).

Someone said that music is the language of heaven. In marriage we can experience a taste of those heavenly sounds when we come to places of acceptance and forgiveness and safety and peace with one another. There is no one on earth with whom I experience such relational intimacy, and that is a taste of heaven itself.

Moments of profound joy, deep satisfaction, and restful peace are like beautiful music that lingers in our minds, preserving the memory, feeding our souls. God is mysterious, touching, moving, present not for moments but forever. And so is my role as helper in all of these things to my husband.

- Refocus on Scripture and see where it leads you in your noble calling as a wife.

- Remember marriage is holy, even on days when it feels hollow.

- Never forget, God is unchanging; His words are eternally true.

I love each of you very much,
Mom

CHAPTER 5

I've already been informed. Get ready. There will be dancing at Laura's wedding. She's definitely her mother's daughter—as a teenager, I mastered the twist, the mashed potato, and other elementary-level dances. Are you impressed? My best girlfriend and I would practice the jitterbug together, and if she wasn't available, I practiced alone by holding the doorknob of my closed bedroom door. In my freshman year of college I dated a guy for several months just because he was a great dancer. I had high standards, for sure.

A year later I became a Christian and everything changed. I stopped dating boys for their dancing skills, and four years later I married a young man who was very much a non-dancer. On our honeymoon, we danced once, the slow dance style of rocking back and forth from one foot to the other. His lack of skill on the dance floor didn't matter, because I loved him and knew God had called us together, but I had a pretty good idea that my dancing days were over.

As you know from any teams you may have belonged to—dance, cheer, volleyball, soccer—when it goes right, when everyone is in sync and playing their position as designed, the combined execution is a pleasing success. But it rarely goes as planned; mistakes are made, misunderstanding the coach happens, we fail to work as a team.

Sounds a little like marriage, doesn't it? Husband and wife are a team of two, and like any athletic or dance team, we are dependent on one another functioning as designed, playing our part well, for the choreography to work beautifully. I want my marriage dance to win approval from the One who matters most. And I hope you do, too.

FOLLOW THE LEADER

Learning to Dance

Dear Mom,

Thanks for the sound advice about building up your man as a leader . . . but what if I'm failing as a follower? And what if he doesn't seem to really want to lead? How does a girl figure that one out?

Dear daughters,

Frankly, I wasn't a good follower, either, and I, your firstborn type-A mother, still don't follow well all the time. Part of my problem was that I thought I had it figured out when I really didn't.

Several years ago we received our Christmas gift of dancing lessons from all six of you, and I was delighted to my toes! Your dad's response was very subdued. But he was a good sport and was willing to give it a try.

On the first lesson, our kind instructor said, "Rhythm is learned."

Right, I thought skeptically. *Not sure I agree, and I know this man. It's not possible.* But I was proven wrong! After just six lessons, we made noticeable improvement, learning the waltz, rumba, tango, and swing. All very much at a beginner level, but we were learning.

Dancing brought great joy in the moment. Often we'd arrive for our six-o'clock lesson, weary from a long day and burdened with the cares of life. The summer of 2008 was a sad one for our whole family, but when your dad and I focused on our dance lesson and on each other, all else faded away. Learning together, sharing together, *moving in step with each other* closed the door on all else for an hour of lightness.

One cannot dance well unless one is paying close attention to the music and to her partner. When a man and woman are dancing together, they have to learn to work in sync as one—think of the best contestants on TV dance competitions who must practice to perfection their coordinated moves. Even beginners like us learned that each partner has a role in the dance, a specific part to play. Most dances are choreographed for the man to lead, usually going forward; he watches for obstacles, other couples moving near, the distance to the edge of the dance floor. His confident posture gives security to his partner, who follows his lead, usually moving backward. His greater physical strength helps her execute the most beautiful twirls, dips, and spins of each dance so that in time she becomes the focal point, the eye candy of the pair—but only as she learns to trust his leadership and strength. From this basic pattern, each particular dance is learned: the steps, the rhythm, the posture, the connection, the eye contact. As he leads, she must learn to watch closely and sense by touch which direction his body is going to take her in the next step, for communication in dance is nonverbal.

Interestingly, during that summer of classes, we often switched partners, and I found that following was not the same with each man. I'm sure the men discovered that leading was different with each woman, too—a perfect illustration of how each duo (and marriage) is unique. Leading and following are to be custom-tailored by each couple. An entire ballroom of

Is the dance—like a marriage—a performance, a business relationship, or the EXPRESSION OF A *Love Song* between the two?

couples may be dancing the waltz, and those watching might say, "They are all doing the same dance," but what can't be seen are the nuances between couples. What appears effortless required much practice. Each couple has their own style in the ways they relate to one another, the level of creativity they apply, the depth of their connection. Is the dance—like a marriage—a performance, a business relationship, or the expression of a love song between the two?

After thirty-six years of marriage I thought the following part would be easy, but I was wrong. During one lesson, our instructor had the women close their eyes and practice feeling the tension changes in his hands, one on her back and the other holding her hand. Inherent in following his lead is a large measure of trust, which became crystal clear during our eyes-closed lesson. Beautiful dancing is simply not possible if both partners are trying to lead.

During our classes I was humbled to realize I was not a good follower. I was sure he needed my help since I was a better dancer, but when I tried to lead, both physically and verbally, we made more mistakes. But when I focused on responding to my husband's faltering steps and less on helping him lead, I found more joy in our experience and he improved more rapidly. And interestingly, when I centered my attention on following, he was more aware of his mistakes and apologized quickly when I wasn't getting in his way and it was his mistake. *Connection*, our instructors taught us, was the key to success.

Concentrating on each other is usually easy to maintain in courtship days, right? As we fall in love and date, we can hardly think about anything more than the one God has brought into our hearts. Most engaged couples assume it will continue on in the same way all their married life. Sure, they've seen marriages falter and fail, but they think smugly, *Ours won't be like that*. But the reality is this: The distractions of real life pull us away from what is needed to make marriage work as beautifully as a dance—focusing on each other and not neglecting our leading and following roles.

All the beautiful twirls and dips and spins of dancing cannot happen without this connection, this mutual dependence between the one who leads (him) and the one who follows (her). We girls love dancing because we love feeling like a princess on the arm of our prince. But we cannot feel like a princess if we are trying to be the prince. Again, lots of practice is needed to learn the steps, but most important is learning to trust, which makes following easier. Trust is a commodity that must be nurtured in your relationship. Mistakes are to be expected, and they will temporarily threaten your trust in him, but work them through and ultimately don't let your husband's mistakes damage your trust in God, the Creator of your dance.

Another of my favorite verses talks about how Jesus, in every suffering he endured, "kept entrusting Himself to Him who judges righteously" (1 Peter 2:23 NASB). As you move in your marriage dance and learn to depend on God as your Leader, following your husband will be less difficult, not because the circumstances are easier but because your trust in your heavenly Father is growing. With time you will learn how to respond with more grace when he changes direction in your marriage dance. The best dancers keep moving even when one partner makes a misstep. Together they trust each other to correct it on the next step or two. When a wife practices these steps of graceful trust, mistakes can become part of the beautiful whole.

If your man is reluctant to lead in a particular area—say leading your family spiritually, a very common complaint for many wives—or if you're reluctant to follow, start with a quick look at your attitude. Are you letting him try to lead, or are you always correcting him so that he has given up and thinks, *Why try?* Are you frequently making suggestions or dropping hints about what he should be doing? I remember driving home from our dance lessons amazed at how poorly I followed in dancing, which made me wonder if I did the same at home. So during the days after our classes I would remind myself, "Follow," "Let him lead," "Respond," "Be sensitive to his cues." Our dance lessons were much more beneficial to our marriage than I ever would have imagined. And we were in a good place at the time, not struggling with one another.

The bottom line is that he may not be leading because you aren't letting him. It was the lesson I had to learn in our class but also in our daily relationship. Most men will back away if they feel challenged or criticized by their wives. Remember, you can't change him. You can only change yourself, so look inside your heart and then remind him that you love him and want to look to him to lead. Ask him questions about the direction your lives are taking, as a couple, as a family, as parents, as disciples on the journey together—whatever—and find out what he thinks the next step should be. If you disagree, discuss it, but don't press for your way. Venture into trying his. I can promise you he will not lead the way you think he should. But if you trust the sovereignty of God, you can be sure that your husband will lead you in the way God designed him to lead you and your family. Eventually, it becomes easier and easier, like a dance you've long practiced.

And maybe you could invest in six dance lessons and have dinner together afterward to discuss the nuances of leading and following? Dance is a beautiful picture of what God intended. Two who are moving through life, arm-in-arm, face-to-face, in step with one another, creating a pattern of beauty and joy.

Remember:

- Every couple is unique.
- Marriage is a beautiful waltz, but one has to lead and the other follow.

- Ultimately, following is a heart attitude that trusts God, the Choreographer.

May your marriage be a beautiful dance to the music of your love,
Mom

P.S. I know Ephesians 5 doesn't say specifically "Husbands, lead your wives," but learning the design of what I do as a woman and what he does as a man in our marriage isn't built on one passage in the Bible alone. The implication from multiple verses in the entire Bible is that as Christ is the head of the church and her Leader, so is the husband to his wife. It is a pattern that cannot be learned in one easy lesson or in one short book such as this, which is why I have continued to point each of you back to Christ as your Master. Listen to what His Spirit says in the whole counsel of Scripture more than you listen to the voices of our culture, which quote a verse here and there but too often out of context or as if all answers are found in one verse. Be wise, my daughters. Listen to the Spirit of God.

Becoming the Star of Your Duo

Dear Mom,

Look, I know it's worked for you and Dad. I'm happy for you. Honestly. I smile just thinking about the two of you. But in today's society, and in my own contemporary marriage, I'm having a really hard time with the idea of submitting to the Hubs. As if I'm lower than he is! I'm sorry, but that just doesn't fly with me. . . . I think we can make it work. Just differently than you and Dad did. Can you still bless that?

My daughter (and her sisters),

Like fingernails on a chalkboard, submission has grated women for centuries. You aren't the first to question its legitimacy. But from four decades of marital experience, I have to say I think you have the wrong idea about what it really means. It's not a domineering, legalistic marriage like those we might observe in strict religions or cults. It's not supposed to take away your identity in some way or make you less-than. Please understand that biblical submission isn't the equivalent of burying a woman in a burka, with only her eyes exposed. We Westerners often look down at our Eastern sisters, feeling pity toward them, wondering how they can survive in that hot tent of fabric and why on earth they would agree to wear it at all.

Think with me for a second. Wouldn't you agree it's plausible that every culture, in every generation, believed some false presuppositions that became normal thinking? The world was once supposed to be flat, remember? Misconceptions are like a thick veil, similar to a burka, which symbolizes an oppressive approach to marital relations, while here in the West female superiority reflects the opposite. But I wonder if we've donned our own sort of veil, and can only see dimly what was once clear. Did you know there is a new "syndrome" today? It's called the Superior Wife Syndrome. Simply put, it's an attitude of condescension many women nurture in relation to their husbands. She feels smarter, more efficient, more capable than the lout she is married to. Too often she takes over and then resents her husband for not doing enough. The dance has died.

To be clear, I think burkas represent an extremely negative view of marriage; I believe they are as repulsive to God as they are to us. But we've come to think of submission as a sort of burka-donning burden. And here is where I think we've begun to see life through our own veil—in our perceptions, and therefore our *feelings* about submission. We have been conditioned to feel it is degrading, subservient, or beneath our dignity. Even the word *role* is viewed negatively, as if being a wife is nothing more than following a script in a play.

Part of our mistaken perception about submission is that it is all about what I have to give up—as if being the leader in the dance is inherently superior, while the follower is inherently inferior. But in fact, true biblical leadership elevates the woman in marriage to a place of importance and development she could not have achieved if she were leading or co-leading with her husband. Think of the couples who make the cut in dance competitions. Which one of the two has the more beautiful moves, the most impressive costume, the preeminent position? It is the woman who is featured, who is lifted high by her partner, who becomes the star of the performance. But she achieves her glory by the long-practiced work of trusting and following her partner. And so it is in marriage, as Paul wrote to his Corinthian children, the woman is the glory of man, but only in relationship to him (see 1 Corinthians 11:7). Context matters.

In reality, submission is not what place I've been put in, but rather what I do *for* my husband. It is a positive choice I make that is supportive and liberating for both of us. It makes the beautiful dance of marriage possible. I let him be a man, a leader, a provider (or primary provider if he is able), all of which God created him to do. I choose to grant him that lead role, to assume ultimate direction for our marriage dance and family dynamics, with lots of information, conversation, and help from me. He is not a dictator, but a fully informed leader of our dance. And when he doesn't have to fight me for his leadership, he is then free to help me become all God intended. Through a husband's sacrificial, loving leadership, his wife becomes the glory of their union.

Like our dancing lessons, there are times I still think my way is better than his, and I have to remind myself where I find the rhythm and ease of movement again. Ultimately, following your husband is a heart attitude that submits to God's design as the Choreographer of marriage.

I have a friend who lives in Alaska. She is married and the mother of three homeschooled children. She also sews, cooks from scratch, and tends beautiful flower gardens. Are you imagining an old-fashioned 1940s woman with an apron tied around her tiny waist? Not this woman! Donna packs a gun, hauls heavy equipment at their lodge, cans and freezes great quantities of food for the long dark winter, and manages a long list of tasks most of us, men or women, can't imagine. She even worked for ten years (before children) on a fishing boat in the Bering Sea. She is one of the strongest—physically, emotionally, mentally, spiritually—women I know. And yet she has decided to let her husband lead.

Femininity is a matter of the heart, as is submission. Donna follows God's design, then her husband's lead. Did you catch that order? First she is a follower of God, then of her husband. Her heart is what makes her feminine, not because she performs certain tasks. The fact that she can defend herself against a grizzly bear with a gun does not make her less feminine. She has a legitimate bias against pampered women who feel marriage is all about satisfying their needs, saying she has learned from Jesus that marriage is not about her, but is about serving and cooperating with her husband, Paul, each doing what they do best, to make a better union of two than they would alone. Donna has embraced submission in her marriage by submitting first to her God, whom she trusts with her

ULTIMATELY following your husband is a heart attitude that submits to God's Design as the Choreographer of Marriage.

By all the laws both of logic and simple arithmetic, to give yourself away in love to another would seem to mean that you end up with less of yourself left than you had to begin with. But the miracle is that just the reverse is true. . . . To give yourself away in love to somebody else—as a man and a woman give themselves away to each other at a wedding—is to become for the first time yourself fully. To live not just for yourself alone anymore but for another self, to whom you swear to be true . . . is in a new way to come fully alive.

—Dr. Frederick Buechner, *Listening to Your Life*

life. Even in the years before Paul came to know Christ and did not lead well, she kept praying, trusting, and following the God who sees all.

Theirs is a different marriage dance than Dennis's and mine, but it is as beautiful as the lupines, columbines, and lobelia that grow with abandon at their lodge. That is God's intent, to have millions of unique husband-and-wife pairs around the world helping others recognize His creative genius.

I'm sure you've heard as I have that submission was just a cultural pattern in biblical times, and therefore we are exempt. I disagree, and here is why: Christ gave His life to see His bride, each of us who belongs to Him, grow and flourish, but He does not force Himself on us. Both men and women must respond and submit to His leading to become everything we were created to be. It is not accidental that the Bible refers to believers as the bride. Again, marriage is a picture of the relationship of the Trinity and a picture of our relationship with Jesus. Therefore, what we saw in the

Old Testament and in Bible times, flawed though it may have been, was still an attempt to follow God's pattern for marriage.

This definition from John Piper explains the concept better than I can:

> Biblical submission for the wife is the divine calling to honor and affirm her husband's leadership and help carry it through according to her gifts. . . . God loves his people and he loves his glory. Therefore when we follow his idea of marriage we are most satisfied and he is most glorified.

Of course, this works best when leading husbands seek to love their wives as Christ loved the church—with everything in them, even willing to die for them. . . . As sinful people, we inevitably fall short on *both* sides of the marriage dance, but like Jesus our Leader, we must keep hoping for the restorative grace He gives.

How grateful I am that women in the West are not forced into burkas. But we must be alert to veiled thinking of a different kind, modern thinking that is opposed to the whole counsel of God's Word. The question for you and me is, Where are we not seeing clearly?

I want a beautiful marriage dance without tripping and falling, which means I have to follow Dennis's leading. If I do, the beauty of our well-practiced dance will bring joy and hope to those watching.

Dancing tips:

- Your heart attitude toward God's design is step one. Submit to God first.

- Step two is relinquishing your desire to lead, sometimes daily.

- Step three: Following my husband's faltering steps encourages him to try harder. When he improves, I win, for we are a dance team for life.

Still learning to follow,
Mom

Refusing a Bad Dance

Dear Mom,

How's the following going, you ask? Yeah. Notsomuch. How's that for an answer? But what am I supposed to do, exactly, when my husband is leading me into territory that I don't think is healthy or holy? And he won't listen?

Dear daughters,

You bring up a challenging question, both in discernment and follow-through. Let's back up again. I painted you a pretty picture in those six dance lessons Dennis and I took. But if you had been there to watch, you would have enjoyed many laughs. Happily, we weren't the only novices in the room, bumbling through one step and then another. But the key is this—when we weren't dancing the way we were supposed to, we allowed the instructors to step in and teach us anew. They showed us the right way, and we attempted to imitate them again. And the question we have to ask ourselves in the marriage dance is this: Is my husband leading me to a place I just can't see (and it makes me nervous or afraid), or do I think he's not following the Instructor's teaching at all? There is a big difference.

Like the intricate steps of a dance, the art of allowing your husband to lead and following that lead by faith is not without risks. It can even be frightening at times, because following any leader involves the unknown. Most of the time I see what is coming in our marriage because we communicate about virtually everything, but as in ballroom dancing, sometimes it's another duo who is suddenly in your way, just as unexpected interruptions or circumstances come into your life and marriage. The one who follows must be alert to respond to a sudden turn in direction. Not being in sync can be costly.

What makes following a challenge for me is the individual decision in which *I want to be right*, because I think he is wrong, or because the particular direction for our family is one *I want to control*. What might be difficult for me in my marriage might be easy for you in yours. It all depends on our personal values, and is complicated by our baggage—those fears and thinking patterns from our backgrounds—and our sinful selfish desires I wrote about earlier. Both spouses can be high control in any given situation, which makes leading and following a challenge.

So given that each situation is layered with complexity, what if you do feel your husband is steering you onto an unhealthy or unholy dance floor? The starting-point truth is that a woman should never follow her husband into sin—like following his request to lie, cheat, view pornography, enter into illicit sexual situations, dishonor his or your parents, or break the law in some way. A husband who is willfully choosing sin is making grave mistakes, and when he asks his wife to join him, she must refuse. That kind of following is not required. A woman who makes "a claim to godliness" (1 Timothy 2:10 NASB) must follow Christ first; Jesus will never ask you to choose sin, even if it requires you to take a step away from your husband for a time. But even in this terrible circumstance, a wife can still have an attitude that seeks to honor her husband, while expressing deep sadness over his choices. People have value apart from their actions.

Remind your husband of your love and commitment to him, but always seek to choose right over wrong, God's way over sin, and encourage him to do the same. Put ultimate trust in God. It was what Esther did in helping her husband avoid the sin of murder. She continued to believe God even in facing potential death at her husband's hand. It's what Peter meant when he wrote of "the holy women who hoped in God" (1 Peter 3:5).

Isaiah 33:6, "And he will be the stability of your times," is a favorite of mine, for it speaks to the One who is constant even when circumstances in a marriage or in the world scream distress. Following in marriage is first of all a heart to follow God, so hear me in this—if he doesn't respond to your encouragement and God's to get back onto a healthy and holy dance floor, it is then time to seek out a godly counselor. There are amazing people out there who can help you with any issue you face and help you get back on track. Ultimately, as a wife, let God use the example of your own life, trusting God supremely to convince your husband to reconsider his ways.

No husband is perfect. Every husband will make decisions that will impact his family negatively. His decisions may have cost your family financially. Maybe his decision resulted in broken relationships with friends or family. The cost could have been emotional or even physical. Your husband can't see in 360 degrees, which means he can't make perfect decisions. Most husbands are good-hearted men who don't intend to cause their wives or children harm or suffering. But following an imperfect man, which all married women must do, means there will be difficult circumstances and some suffering as a result. Still, God is saying, "Do you believe my design is very good? Will you trust me?" Or is He saying to you, "This is a dangerous, unholy path. Step away and call to your husband, remind him of your love, and pray the truth will be revealed to him"?

In the "worst of times" in any marriage, wives must be more supportive, more on guard, more alert than in ordinary times. Peter says our behavior can win our husbands. I know many women who risked believing God's Word and had to step away from their husbands for years or even for the rest of their lives; I've also known many others who have experienced the miracle of a resurrected marriage and a new man for a husband, like my friend Donna, who I wrote about in the last letter. Nothing is impossible with God.

Women are powerful. Don't doubt how God is directing you if He's igniting alarm in your heart about sin. Stand strong and true.

But also remember that your husband is still growing, and God is nurturing him to become "an oak of righteousness." Learning to lead takes years and years. You can help by encouraging his leadership and praying that that continues, throughout your life together, even if he gets off track for a time. Patience is abundant with God, but sadly, we wives possess a shallow supply.

Steps to get back on the right dance floor:

- Step one: Make sure your heart is right, that you are trusting and submitting to God's holy work in you, first.

- Step two: Make sure your behavior reflects that ultimate trust in God and doesn't demonstrate fear or panic or criticism for your husband.

- Step three: If he doesn't respond to your godly behavior, seek the wisdom of a skilled counselor.

Still, *still* learning to follow,
Mom

COOPERATIVE DANCE PARTNERS
A Tango Over Gymnastics

Dear Mom,

So let me get this straight. Are you saying you follow all of Dad's decisions? Like, do you really talk stuff through? Or is following and the submission thing just agreeing with him because you know God is ultimately in control? It just gives me a headache trying to understand how it works.

Hello, girls,

This leading-and-following topic requires lots of conversation and communication over decades to find a place of comfort and ease in the dance of marriage. I do not pretend to say it is easy or that I understand it all. Writing these letters gave me a headache, trying to make plain what is a mystery!

First, let me say there are people who look at Dennis and me and mistakenly think he leads our marriage with dictatorial authority because he is a strong leader of others, and that I simply follow what he says. Assumptions are easy to make about others when we look from afar and don't have the facts. But the truth for us is your dad is an incredibly patient listener who wants to lead me fully informed. As a result, there have been only a handful of times when we disagreed on a decision and I ended up reluctantly submitting to your dad's direction, as unto the Lord. "As unto the Lord" is an important distinction, which I'll get to.

Again, the model for the marriage relationship is Jesus and His relationship with us. He does not force His will on any of us. He leads us with love and grace. Likewise, your dad, even with his flaws and failures, has prayed and worked and learned to lead me the same way as much as he can. Even so, there have been a few times when we could not agree on a decision, and as the leader of our family who must answer to God for the direction our family takes, your dad asked me to follow him and his decision even though I disagreed.

One of those situations happened about twenty years ago. We were battling each other over a decision, and neither of us offered any compromise. We were diametrically opposed.

The issue was whether or not to let you, Rebecca, continue on to level seven in gymnastics. I loved watching you perform, delighting in your lithe little body that bent and tumbled with such grace and beauty. Visions of the Olympics, of college scholarships, of medals and awards tumbled in my head. Clearly God had given you a gift. He had made you more flexible than most on your team. *He must have a great plan for the future,* I thought. And I was excited just thinking about it.

But a cost was being paid for your achievements. Beyond the escalating financial investment, an investment of time was also being made—a forty-five-minute one-way commute, four three-hour sessions a week, and weekend meets. Hidden in the fine print was a relational cost. And here is where your dad and I had a serious disagreement.

He was increasingly concerned about the amount of time you were spending with coaches compared with time at home with us. Because gymnastics is a year round sport, the coaches and other team members could have a greater influence in your life than we would. That was a red flag for him.

For three long months we discussed the same facts. Over and over he expressed concern about the time and influence factors. Over and over I said, "What if we are wasting her potential that God gave her? Maybe God wants her to go to the Olympics. What if she resents us for taking her out of something she loves? Okay, so maybe not the Olympics, but she could get a college scholarship and we

> Over and over, Shakespeare explored the same theme [of love], following the same rigid rules: 14 lines, iambic pentameter, set rhyme scheme. Those tight restraints unleashed the Bard's mighty power, such as the world has never seen.
>
> —Karen Swallow Prior

could use the money." I thought the money angle would work, but not this time.

Our discussions flipped back and forth like your beautiful tumbling across the floor exercise mat. You could execute up to ten back handsprings in a row without stopping, and we matched every one in each discussion. And neither of us changed position.

Finally, I wearied of our lack of resolution. It seemed we talked about nothing else, and it was affecting our marriage. At the end of one of our weekly date nights, again dominated by this conversation, I decided one of us had to give up the fight. My understanding of the biblical pattern for marriage reminded me I had a choice to follow, to trust that God was leading through your dad. So I told him I'd follow his lead regardless of how I felt. And then I prayed God would show him he was wrong.

The next day God gave me a peace that this was right. When your dad explained our decision, you had no hesitation about quitting, which surprised me. The freedom from the hours spent in the car was greater than I ever imagined, and I thought, *Wow, God, you know what you're doing!*

This was a pivotal moment for me in our marriage, as I saw God leading so clearly through your dad for my good and for Rebecca's good. It was as if we'd been at opposite ends of a line dance for those months; then suddenly the music changed and we were partners again, dancing eye to eye and with an ease we hadn't had in a long long time. You see, what made this difficult decision work so well was that it was "unto the Lord," a biblical phrase that simply means my decision to follow was in the context of a spiritual reality that is far greater than my little marriage. The bottom line is I trusted God more than I trusted my husband. I believed He was big enough to change my husband if he was wrong, or He would change me if I was wrong. So ultimately I was open to God's doing what He needed to do.

Following in marriage, which includes both trusting and submitting, is ultimately about cooperation with each other and with God. I am willing to follow because I trust the pattern; I submit to the order God has established for making a marriage dance move beautifully. We are in this relationship together for life. I have learned that your dad has my best interests at heart and wants good for me. Even when he makes selfish decisions—which are increasingly rare—they are never intended to harm me or cause me pain. Because I believe God's pattern is worth the risk of following, I want to cooperate with him, to work together in harmony; therefore, most of the time following is not that hard. Practice doesn't make perfect, but it does make it easier.

Watching Rebecca tumble was a season of joy and delight in my life. A gift of grace. But moving in harmony with the music God writes with my husband is of far greater value, because our relationship is not for a season but for life. Our dance must be preeminent.

Tips for decision making:

- Boldly but respectfully share your perspective, intuition, fears, and hopes with your husband about the decision on which you don't yet agree.

- Do it more than once if needed, but make sure you are willing to hear his side.

- If you can't agree, you must trust your husband and God's sovereign rule to change him if he is wrong. Then watch and see what God does!

Much love and hugs,
Mom

Advanced Lessons

Dear Mom,

So what do I do if I am really more the "natural leader"? It's easier and quicker for me to make decisions, while he is slower. I mean, he takes L O T S of time to gather info, Mom! Plus, one of his gifts is harmonizing with people. So he's always asking tons of people for their opinion and advice. Sometimes it drives me crazy, like why can't the two of us just do this thing? I could have gotten us there so much faster!

Dear daughters,

Without question there are millions of marriages in which it seems a mistake has been made when it comes to who has the leadership skills and who gets to be the leader. Another mistaken assumption about your dad and me is that I'm quiet and reserved, and therefore following is easy for me and leading is easy for your dad. NOT! Maybe I should have Dennis weigh in here about the challenges of leading a strong perfectionist woman who is very much like her father, who didn't tolerate mistakes well. Leading me has not been a cakewalk. As I said earlier, there have been plenty of times when I felt my way was superior to his, and he felt that critical attitude from me.

But doesn't this leading-following pattern show up in all of life, in all relationships? Every day in hundreds of ways we each are submitting to, trusting, and following a complex system of rules in the greater dance of life. For instance, when you get in your car every single day, you agree to abide by the rules of the road. Viewing from a helicopter, you might even see the swirl of traffic as a kind of dance. Cars stop and turn and curve and yield the right of way on the dance floor of your town. Most of us don't think twice about yielding the right of way to another driver when signage tells us to; it's just like submitting to the rules of dance. The laws of driving allow for our safety and the smooth ebb and flow of traffic. But without rules, being in traffic is truly frightening—like the time we rode in a taxi in Egypt years ago. With no traffic lights or traffic signs, every driver did what was right in his own eyes, bullying his way through the congestion by constantly blaring his horn. Without ordered rules and without respect for that order, it was a free-for-all. And so it is in marriage. Someone with far greater intelligence, who also cares about our safety and well-being, choreographed the steps for the marriage dance. If we could see this pattern from the vantage of a heavenly helicopter, it, too, would make much more sense. It is respect for His design that creates peace and order.

Perhaps you are a more "natural" leader, but do you think God might have something for you to learn from cooperating with your man, who in your eyes isn't as gifted as you? And are you so sure your evaluation is correct? Might you both have leadership ability, but you are valuing yours over his because you are different? Are you sure you are seeing it all so clearly?

In our fallen ness we are too prone to think we know more than God. Our sister Eve fell for the bait that God had something she didn't and that she deserved to know what He knew. We think we are wiser than she, but we are no different at all. Another of my favorite Bible stories is when Peter saw John and wanted to know what his destiny was, so he asked Jesus, "What about this man?" Jesus replied, "If it is my will that he remain until I come, *what is that to you? You follow me!*" (John 21:22, emphasis added). Your husband is who God gave you, and He knows what He is doing. "You follow me," Jesus says to you, too!

In every marriage since the beginning of time, God has choreographed thousands and thousands of details for purposes we cannot envision. Perhaps your friend's husband seems so much kinder and gentler than yours, but I would say in reply, "Do you know what happens behind closed doors

where you can't see?" Oh, you just read a blog about a young husband who said he is thrilled over his wife's book that just came out, and you can't find the time to even write in your journal? And I would ask, "Does a book indicate success? Do you know what had to go undone, what needs in her children were unmet, what relational costs were paid?" You have no idea, right? I find it intriguing that we don't look at the young wife who has stage-four cancer and wish for her life. As Jesus said to Peter, "What is that to you? You follow me." Learn to respect the unseen purposes that God wants to work for your good and His glory in *your* marriage. Learn to respect *your* God-given man in all his limitations. Ask God to show you the beauty of your man's strengths and gifts and talents. This is advanced-level dancing, finding the uniquenesses in your man and in your marriage and respecting them instead of wishing them away.

In our marriage I have learned to accept the fact that I don't see things as objectively as my husband, and as a result I regularly ask him for his opinion on most decisions.

God choreographed

In every marriage since the beginning of time,
God has choreographed thousands and thousands of details
for purposes we cannot envision.

Not because I can't think for myself, but because I want a sounding board, to hear his thinking, his perspective; many times I want his approval. Again, not because I'm incapable, but because I value his perspective; over the years I've learned how important it is to me in so many ways. It's also a foundational way I show him respect. He knows I value him when I ask for his thoughts. And he asks me for my opinion on most every decision he makes. He trusts my female intuition. He knows I see and hear things in conversations that he totally misses. He knows my heart is to follow Christ and that the advice I give will be wise and godly, not self-serving. We help each other make decisions as a team. I respect him, I value his opinion, I want his involvement in my life, and he respects me and my perspective. We are partners in this journey. We balance each other.

Recently I made a decision not to follow his advice, and it cost me dearly. We were involved in a situation with some friends where some feelings had been hurt. I was more upset emotionally than my husband was, and I wrote an email to this person expressing how I felt, and then asked my husband to read what I had written. He read it and said, "I don't think you should send it. I'd wait." So I waited, but only about two hours. The longer I waited, the more angry I became, and finally I decided I didn't care and hit the send button.

I was deceived by my emotions. I believed I was right, but a few days later I discovered my husband was the wiser in this instance. Our friend felt judged by my words. I had apologies to make and broken fences to repair. And I learned never to send an email that was emotionally charged again without my husband agreeing. It felt good in the moment to say what I really felt, but afterward it was bitter. So is the nature of sin.

I'm more confident than ever that God knew what He was doing when He designed this plan of leading and following in marriage. Someday it will make perfect sense. But today it is still a mystery, a mystery to be lived, not solved. Great faith is required for a woman to allow her husband to lead, and then to follow that direction. A man also exercises great faith as he learns to listen to God and waits for his wife to follow cooperatively and helpfully. His job isn't nearly as easy as we think it is.

In the end, it is God who will carry you when your husband trips and stumbles or when life requires a more difficult dance. And it is God who will help your husband when you resist and make his leading difficult. Keep on dancing, because He will never leave you or abandon you. And that is reason enough.

You aren't a beginner anymore, so:

- Demonstrate great faith by daily giving thanks for your man.

- Give him the gift of respect for who he is today, knowing your gift will free him to become the leader God knows you need tomorrow.

- Invite his perspective, opinion, and advice. Though he is not infallible, there will be truth in what he says. Ask God to help you listen well.

Love always,
Mom

P.S. Respect him even when it doesn't make sense, because it is right. Jesus said, "Give, and it will be given to you." The gift of respect is a principle of the upside-down kingdom that Jesus introduced, a kingdom full of surprise and paradox. And so it is true in marriage.

NEW SEASONS AND NEW NEEDS
Changing Rhythms

For all the various metaphors in these letters about dancing, I've decided that they are not just illustrative but factual. God is the Divine Choreographer. *Sovereignty* and *providence* are two big words we use to describe God's intimate involvement with His people. So to describe life and marriage as a dance is not a stretch at all. Though our marriages are all fraught with mistakes and missteps, we two who begin as novices, as little more than babes, can learn to dance together beautifully and lightly if we nurture hearts that remain open to the Master Instructor. It is a worthy goal, which is necessary if we want to arrive at the end firmly united as a couple. But the road is not easy.

The daily truth about our marriages is that often we move in disunity. We do not have perfect knowledge that leads to the understanding necessary for constant peace. Additionally, we coexist with varying levels of tension that bubble to the surface from our differences, weaknesses, and needs. Like suddenly being asked to learn a new dance after finally feeling we've mastered one, we are usually threatened by new discoveries in our marriage, in ourselves, and in our spouse. The dance we grew comfortable with has changed. But remaining willing to learn opens the door to a deeper understanding of one another and can result in a new level of mutual appreciation. It is what we married for, this deep dance rhythm that we share with only one. It is a fallacy to imagine we will arrive at mastery. We won't, because that is not His goal for us.

But we resist His instruction. Why? Because we worship comfort and ease and sameness. Life feels safer that way. We think we'd be happier. But it is not the way of God. His goal is to conform us to the image of His Son, which requires ongoing change. He is nudging us to learn new dance steps together, and marriage is one of His favorite tools for doing His purifying work in our hearts. Though in His hand our personhood is in a state of flux, it is good even though it doesn't feel that way. Like my friend Susan Yates says, "Stability is not the norm in life, change is."

Another dear friend, Terri, has been learning a brand-new dance with her husband after he had a stroke and their lives changed drastically. Terri's dance is not yours or mine. She is responsible only for hers. And so are we. Deal with what you've been given, trusting God that He knows what He is doing and will give you all that you need to dance the dance of today.

- Be open to learning new dances with your man.

- Remember that God knows what He is doing even when we can't see where He is leading.

- Welcome new, more intricate steps as you mature together.

May you find beautiful, soul-satisfying comfort as you persevere. Your Dance Instructor will always, always guide you if you let Him.

With love,
Mom

P.S. Recently I drove to Camden to take my mom, your grandmother, to dinner for her eighty-eighth birthday. Granted, this is a southern town, but as we were walking into the restaurant, a mother and her son were walking out the door. This young man of about ten or eleven years old on his own initiative stopped and held the door open for my mother and me to enter. In that moment we had a choice. We could have refused his kindness and told him to come on out. (And I know of women who have felt deeply insulted by a man who wanted to express honor by this gentle-manly action.) But truly there was no choice in my mind. To refuse would have been rude. We smiled at him, walked in, and I thanked him for his kind, thoughtful, self-sacrificing act on our behalf. I very much wanted to affirm his courtesy, because it is a step toward his becoming the kind of man who will make a very good husband one day.

Those of you who have sons are training them to become husbands. Giving them doses of respect, admiring them as they learn to lead and serve others, calling out the best in them are crucial ways you can cooper-ate with God's hand as He forms them into the men He desires them to be for the unique plans He has for them.

Here is a very practical, God-designed biological fact about men, which is also true of your sons, that deserves our respect, even though it can drive us crazy sometimes. *Most* men—I'm sure there are rare exceptions—are

When we trust the Choreographer, we move with GREATER freedom, fulfillment, and beauty.

wired to be more objective than women, primarily because their brains can compartmentalize their thinking more easily. Which explained to me, when I finally understood, why when your dad was reading the paper or working on the computer, he didn't always hear you kids fighting in the same room. Our female brains are more like a circling radar, where we are juggling multiple agendas and tasks at once while knowing where everyone is in the house at any given moment. We are different, and different is not wrong, remember?

This biology lesson has applications to leadership. We lead with different perspectives and with different sets of data as men and women. My highly tuned radar is a gift to my husband, who lacks this female trait. He frequently wants to know what I think, what I hear, and what I see because he knows I take in far more information than he does in any given situation. His ability to focus and stick to the facts is good for me, too. It's another way we work as a team, combining our strengths to make a stronger union.

A favorite author of mine, Anne Morrow Lindbergh, wrote this about marriage:

> A good relationship has a pattern like a dance and is built on some of the same rules. The partners do not need to hold on tightly, because they move confidently in the same pattern, intricate but gay and swift and free, like a country dance of Mozart's. . . . There is no place here for the possessive clutch, the clinging arm . . . because they know they are partners moving to the same rhythm, creating a pattern together, and being invisibly nourished by it.
>
> *Gift From the Sea*

So in our marriage today, we move in harmony most of the time because we have practiced our dance and have valued what we each bring to our marriage. Marriage has a pattern that was divinely designed for our good and His glory. When we trust the Choreographer, we move with greater freedom, fulfillment, and beauty. And it is very good.

Marriage
IS LIKE A
Secret Garden

CHAPTER 6

Gardening is in my blood. I've wondered if the smell of earth, the satisfaction of tending the ground, the nurturing of life from its darkness are memories from the original garden, or if they are part of the genetic material I received from grandparents and great-grandparents who tilled the same soil for over one hundred years. Regardless, the longing to create beauty with bordered beds and brilliant colors has long pulled me out the door of my house on many sunny days (along with a need to escape the chaos of kid-land). Weeding a flowerbed that stayed tidy for a week or two, as opposed to cleaning my ever-messy kitchen, gave me a sense of accomplishment. Reclaiming the wild and establishing order was a taste of redemption in my otherwise constantly disordered life. Being outside, getting my hands in the soil, moving rocks, and making beautiful borders fed my soul with the nourishment of sunshine and fresh air.

Over the thirty years that we've lived in this house on

our sunset-view ridge, we've managed to gradually turn our rock- and weed-covered property into quite a beautiful sight. It's been a very slow process, interrupted by kids and travel and lack of funds. My gardens have also endured damage from torrential rains that carved little rivers through my nicely manicured beds; flowers and plants stomped to death by little feet, dogs and cats, chickens and deer; and most recently, significant destruction from the tornado that leveled over two dozen mature pine and oak trees onto fences and decks, crushing rose beds and dogwood trees, and uprooting huge chunks of our sidewalk and once-manicured zoysia grass.

Creating a garden of beauty is not for the faint of heart, and neither is marriage. It is inestimably harder than I ever expected. And what I thought before marriage would be the easiest part of all—sex—has proven to be one of the most difficult aspects over the decades of our relationship. I'm grateful for the opportunity to write you these letters. I would never be able to say all this in person, even to my biological daughters . . . not just because I have a lot to say, but because even with a healthy relationship, these matters are simply not always easy to chat about face-to-face.

UNDERSTANDING THE PURPOSE AND IDEAL OF SEX

A Lock and Key

Dear Mom,

So, yeah. Sex. You gave me "the talk," and we had our pre-wedding conversation that was pretty short and hurried. No offense; it was busy. I get it. But now I'm married. And it's um . . . different. Fine. FINE. But, well, I have to ask this . . . what's the big deal?

Daughters of mine,

You make me smile. Oh, how I understand, well . . . I think I understand what you are feeling and thinking!

Do you remember Mary Lennox in *The Secret Garden*? That book was one of our favorites. For those who haven't read it, it's the story of little Miss Mary, born in India, orphaned at nine, and sent to live with an eccentric uncle, Mr. Craven, at his huge estate in England, a cold, wet, and dreary world. There were no other children to play with, or so Mary thought, so she began to explore her new surroundings. Roaming the finely kept grounds day after day, she unexpectedly discovered to her delight a secret garden with ivy-covered walls eight feet high and intriguing garden beds and pathways, though badly overgrown with weeds. The joy of the story is watching a lonely little girl grow and blossom as she nurtures life back into the garden beside two unexpected friends, Dickon and Colin. With dedicated, loving care, the secret garden became lovely once again.

Like Mr. Craven's large estate, our marriages have many visible walkways and rooms where others may be welcomed for conversation and interactions. But as the secret garden at Misselthwaite Manor had a door with a lock and key, so marriages have a private space that none may enter but two. Sex is that hidden place where husband and wife can nurture the life-giving joy and contentment God intended sexual pleasure to provide. It is a place of retreat, comfort, and trusted safety built by love. As Mary said to herself of the garden, "It's like being shut out of the world in some fairy place." This, too, is what God intended in the beginning.

Sex is the holiest place in marriage. We come near to the oneness of God Himself when we are there. There is something very mysterious, something beyond comprehension in our physical unity. Being abandoned in complete trust to each other and experiencing pleasure like none other is somehow a taste of what will be in heaven. The depth of love, the purity of joy, the setting aside of shame will be ours not just for fleeting seconds, but for eternity with Christ. We honor Him when we protect our union. When we are faithful to one another, we say, "Betrayal of His sacrifice will not happen in this house, nor will we belittle His redemptive work by

treating our marriage and our sexual union lightly or as unholy." Commitment to always pursue deeper oneness protects us from hard hearts toward God and each other.

One of our private conversations over the length of our marriage, which I share with permission, is my husband's compliment of me when he says, "Thanks for making me more effective at work." Sex is energizing for a man. When he is received and welcomed by his wife, he feels he can conquer the world. Or at least face the challenges before him that day! My husband knows I respect his manhood, that I love him enough to make this part of our marriage important. What he is saying to me is that he is free to go to work without being burdened by unfulfilled needs between us. Yes, there have been times when he's gone to work with unmet needs and unresolved conflict between us. We are two sinful people. But over the years he's learned I am for him, on his team. He understands this in part by my commitment to our mutually fulfilling sex life.

The secret garden of marriage is a place of raw exposure that God can use as a sacred space of redemption.

unique & distinct

Each marriage—like one's own garden—
is unique and distinct from all others, reflecting
the beauty of God's individual handiwork.

When we take our clothes off, we are exposing far more than our physical bodies. It's as if our ability to hide falls on the floor with the clothing. Our shame, fears, and flaws we conceal so well by day seem to be all over our skin by night. And in this way, sex is far more complex than a mere physical act. Our insecurities ask, "Will you still love me if you know or see this?" They clamor to be hidden again, and we wish we could dismiss them easily, but they must be named and exposed to each other. Will you be forgiven, will you be understood, will you still be loved? And he needs the same. One by one, over and over, fears and shame must be revealed in order to be replaced by truth and love. In facing each other in the safety of this hidden place, we can experience the acceptance for which we long.

It is one of the reasons God created this safe place for couples. Inside the garden with the door locked, we can discover renewal, rebirth, refreshment.

And that is what God's truth spoken through us will do: remove the old ideas, beliefs, and fears so that I can put on the new, "a heart of compassion, kindness, humility, gentleness and patience" (Colossians 3:12 NASB). If I love my husband, then I will want to know him completely, and in that knowing to understand and have empathy so I can love more. My goal is to help him be all God intended, to not be a hindrance in his life, and to allow him to do the same for me. In the safety of a committed marriage, the miracle of healing and wholeness by the Spirit of God works its redemption power slowly . . . step by step . . . over time. By faith we persevere, knowing each marriage—like one's own garden—is unique and distinct from all others, reflecting the beauty of God's individual handiwork.

And there is more.

Like in any well-tended garden, there are always ways to make it more beautiful by adding new plants to the mix or moving others that need more sunlight. Many times I've made the mistake of planting new seedlings in our backyard in a less than optimal location. Slow growth and few blooms tell me the conditions are not right. Understanding our southern climate and what flourishes here has taken years and lots of trial and error.

And so it is with the secret garden of marriage.

Secret gardening tips:

- Protecting our oneness keeps the soil of our hearts tilled and fertile.

- In the safety of our secret garden healing happens.

Hugs,
Mom

Opposite Gardening Zones

Mom,

This is a little embarrassing. Okay, a lot embarrassing. But please tell me that sex is more than I think it is. It's fine. Don't get me wrong. But the initial *cough* passion has pretty much cooled off, we have all the kids we want, and honestly, sex seems like the last thing on my list of needs because I am tired A L L the T I M E!

Dear daughters,

Boy, do I understand you. Dennis always said he'd be a millionaire if he had one dollar for all the times I said how tired I was! And sex was at the bottom of my to-do list more times than not. We missed each other often. Making sense of our sexual differences sometimes felt like we were from two solar systems, not just Venus and Mars. I totally get that time and energy is a huge challenge on this front!

First, a quick sweet story about your grandma: While we were shopping for something to wear for my wedding night, my mother gave me two very brief pieces of advice about sex. As I was trying on a beautiful white eyelet nightgown, she said, "He'll like you much better naked, you know." Then she added, "It gets a lot better with time." She was right about both. While sex can seem automatic and even easy in the beginning, especially since it is so hard to control passion before marriage, becoming great lovers for life is a decades-long learning experience that improves with age. Think of a young oak sapling, just planted; then consider that same tree in maturity, the satisfying shade it provides in summer, the glorious color in autumn, the strength of its limbs through a bitter winter, the continued growth come spring. It helps to remember an oak tree takes decades to mature, and so do our marriages, so work to be patient with one another, okay?

When you girls got married, I remember preparing mentally, thinking through what I wanted to say about sex in marriage. It wasn't that we hadn't talked about sex before, because we'd been very open as parents, but this was a special one-time moment we'd never have again.

One of the topics I tried to explain is how different we are sexually as male and female. In the early months of my marriage, I thought it was only a physical difference. Sex was a relatively simple experience for us. At least it was until we began to encounter some surprisingly distinct differences. Like so many women before me, I discovered that we could have just had an argument, and he could immediately set that aside and be "interested." Or that he didn't need any conversation before being "ready." Or that we would be in the middle of lovemaking and he wouldn't hear the crash just outside our apartment walls! And yes, it is true that not all men are exactly the same. But from the beginning, men were designed by God to think about sex more often and in a more focused way than women. It's the ability to compartmentalize again. A biological and physiological fact.

Even though I've learned a lot about living with a man, I still find myself caught off guard at times by our gender differences. The combination of chromosomes that makes an embryo a boy or a girl keeps us male and female for life on a cellular level. And it never changes. Think about this with me for a second. Most couples would say they

What is hard about marriage is what is hard also about facing the Christian God: it is the strain of living continually in the light of a conscience other than our own, being under the intimate scrutiny of another pair of eyes. It is really judgment that we fear, the sense of being in the glare of a moral searchlight.

—Mike Mason, *The Mystery of Marriage*

have much in common; their basic emotions, education levels, and beliefs can be the same. But for me as a woman, knowing what it is like to be my husband, a man—to crawl inside his skin and feel what he feels—is not possible. I will never think like a man; I will always view the world through estrogen-shaded feminine lenses, while he will always have a testosterone-fueled male view on life.

Marriage has taught me how vastly different the sexes are. When God created woman, He gave her multiple avenues for expressing the essence of her femaleness, her sexuality. Sexual intercourse is one. But the conception of a child and the creation of a new life only take place in a woman's body. Men can merely watch and wonder. After the child is born, a woman can physically nurse the babe for months and even years. A man may feed a baby with a bottle and join in the process of caring for his child, but he will never know the deep fulfillment and satisfaction a woman feels when she nurses her child. Childbearing, nursing, and sustaining the life of a child are profound affirmations of our female sexuality. Women were made to give life. It is an expression of our femaleness even if we never have a biological child. Childless women can still express this essential femininity by nourishing others, and many do in other life-giving ways. We are nurturers by God's design.

But by contrast, a man's sexuality can only be expressed in one way, and that is through sexual intercourse. His masculinity is subjected by the design of the Creator to a brief performance. A woman can participate in intercourse with her husband without having to become aroused. He cannot. One author on the subject bluntly stated:

> His erection is a mysterious endowment that he can never fully understand or control. If it goes [away], he often will not know exactly why, and there will be little he or his partner can do to retrieve it.
>
> George Gilder, *Men and Marriage*

It was enlightening for me to understand that a woman may "need" a man in order for her to get pregnant, but once that is accomplished, she can continue feeling like a woman and not "need" him again, whereas a man "needs" a woman for affirmation of his manhood over and over and over. This is one of the reasons sex is one of the last things on your list of needs. The pH of his soil is very different from yours.

Another epiphany for me came from the same author:

> Unless they have an enduring relationship with a woman—a relationship that affords them sexual confidence—men will accept almost any convenient sexual offer. The existence of a semi-illegal, multibillion-dollar pornography market, almost entirely male-oriented, bespeaks of the difference in sexual character between men and women.

Women are designed to be the stabilizing force in the lives of men. Far from being insignificant, we are instead supremely important. Without the stabilizing commitment of women in marriage, men are more likely to live like barbarians, wandering impulsively through life, fighting, competing, and chasing after power they might not even be able to define. Sadly today, many young men are enjoying the pleasures of marriage without the commitment or responsibility because many young women are too willing to cohabit instead of demanding a marriage proposal by their refusal to give sex outside of marriage. So there might be a temporary stability created in these unmarried couples who cohabit, but it will not last or produce healthy relationships.

WOMEN ARE DESIGNED TO BE THE *stabilizing force* IN THE LIVES OF MEN.

Your dad has often said to me, "Women are powerful," but every time he said it, I never quite comprehended his meaning. Until I read George Gilder's book *Men and Marriage*. Understanding this male-female difference has helped me make sense of my deep, life-altering responsibility to my husband to help him feel like the man God created him to be. And that includes my being willing to learn what says love to him, and his being willing to learn what says love to me. Our needs and desires are sometimes vastly dissimilar, but we have worked together to both compromise and take risks. It is supremely important that you hear this conclusion I came to understand: If I love him, I won't view his biological sexual differences disapprovingly. This is a very practical way you as a wife can and must show him respect. If you belittle or shame his male sexuality, any other attempts at showing respect will feel hollow to him.

As the two of us had conversations about sex and our divergent perspectives in those early years, seeking to know one another better, I caught glimpses of what it must be like to be a man. It was a continual revelation. I felt compassion for him and more motivation to care for him. But within days of each conversation, I returned to viewing life as a woman. Truth is not a magic wand that changes a woman's sex drive into a man's, but it helps correct our misguided thinking. Still, a thousand conversations will not revolutionize my design or his.

We have come to a place after decades of marriage where we understand we will never view sexual intimacy in the same way. For many years we thought cultural conditioning created our differences, but I believe now that male-female differences are God-designed for a purpose. I do not feel a sexual need for him *the same way* he does for me. Hear me clearly on this. I feel that need uniquely as a woman, needing not a physical release as do men, but an emotional filling, the rebonding and reconnection that comes from reaffirming our commitment through sex. There are times when I'm just not in the mood—we girls are emotional beings, right?—and we mutually agree to delay making love until the next night (and sometimes we opt for a quicker method to meet his physical need), but regardless, I make sure he knows I am not *rejecting* him. Why? Because he needs to know I respect his need and personhood as a man. He can feel dismissed and therefore disrespected, so I have learned to protect him by what I say and don't say. Over time we have proven we are for each other. He knows my heart is for him. And he appreciates that my heart must be as wooed as my body. Still, there are times I request being together because I've just missed him, and I feel it, not physically as he, but emotionally. We are different, and it is good.

Sometimes in the midst of everyday life with kids and carpools, lessons and lectures, meetings and messes, I've had to remind myself how important sex is to my husband. Knowing he needs me to nurture beauty and life from his male soil requires that I plan for him and keep my relationship with him my number-one priority. And that isn't always easy. You may "feel," as I often did, a far greater need for sleep than for sex, but your husband's God-given sexual desire is for your good and the good of your marriage. Or if your husband's interest in sex (more on this in another letter) is lacking, you may feel neglected by him, which creates a different kind of marital stress. In either circumstance there is always work to be done and hope for a healthy marriage.

- You will never totally understand what it's like to be male.

- He will never totally understand what it's like to be female.

- Remember, his sexual difference is not a weakness. It's a gift to your relationship.

Thanking God for the genius of His design even when I can't appreciate the wonder,
Mom

P.S. There are additional unseen benefits to regular sexual relations in marriage. Three little facts I learned from one of our *FamilyLife Today* radio guests: The chemicals oxytocin and dopamine, when released in the brain, increase bonding; the reexpression of love and commitment strengthens mutual affection; and there is a sense of satisfaction in keeping intimacy alive even if the actual experience isn't a great one. The last one is my favorite, because in our marriage, sex hasn't always been accompanied by fireworks! Among a lot of good-to-great experiences, we've also had some pretty lousy encounters . . . some that left us both either disappointed or hurt. That makes the chemical facts all the more important, because even not-great sex still bonds us together. Nice to know, huh?

DEALING WITH PRIOR SEXUAL EXPERIENCES
Repairing Broken Branches

Dear Mom,

Without betraying a confidence, I need your help. There are some, ahh, issues in our intimate life stemming from past decisions. Is it just our path to deal with the repercussions of sin and know that it won't ever be as great as if it hadn't happened? Or is there hope for healing?

My sweet daughter (and all her sisters):

There is always, always hope. Cling to that.

Do you remember what Mary Lennox saw when she first entered the door to the secret garden? Piles of leaves, weeds and thistles, broken branches, and rocks and bits of mortar fallen from the walls greeted her eyes. The garden was in terrible disrepair. Yet instead of seeing the ruins as impossible, she saw with wonder what could be. Her eyes saw potential beauty, the hope of new life. Immediately she began her restoration work. Likewise, our sexual relationships are often begun with walls broken and fractured and with the weeds of past experiences choking out healthy sexual expression.

As in Mary's garden, restoration to beauty is possible in the secret garden of marriage. We were made to bloom, to flourish in the place of maximum sunlight with the right amount of moisture, not too little, not too much. God plants us in a marriage with the potential to grow as individuals to mature beauty. But it takes time.

As a boomer-generation child, I came of age in the early days of the sexual revolution. Another friend and radio guest, Dr. Meg Meeker, a pediatrician, said that our generation has left a terrible legacy in the sexual liberation we inaugurated. I agree with her. Casual sex is an epidemic spreading like wildfire, and the implications for the children of this generation are frightening. As a result, it is rare that young couples marry today as virgins or enter matrimony untouched by abuse. Far too often, one or both carry physical, psychological, and emotional sexual scars into marriage. It is a tragic and profound loss for each individual, for the couple, and for the health of our nation.

You all know the story your dad tells about the time when he and I were dating and I refused to let him hold my hand. Two previous relationships that had taken me where I did not want to go convinced me that

no touching was the safest way to avoid further regret. I had learned that allowing any physical involvement with a young man meant opening the door to something difficult to stop, so I told your dad when we were dating I was not interested in any physical expression of affection. I was afraid he'd break up with me, but I think he admired me more for having convictions. After getting married, I began to realize that any prior sexual experience has long-lasting repercussions. Though I knew I was forgiven, two manipulative relationships were enough to leave me with significant regret and a damaged ability to trust, common problems in every marriage with any prior sexual experience. I tell you this to say the consequences were difficult, but with perseverance we have overcome. I understand and have great compassion and grace for those who enter marriage broken like me, and sadly it seems to be the majority today.

I don't envy what your generation faces. The traumas of date rape, sexual assault, sexual abuse, emotional abuse, pornography, STDs, the regret of consensual "safe" sex, abortion . . . I see so many struggling with the repercussions—the depression, the grieving of a loss, even psychological damage. It feels like too much, but I know God is supremely able to rescue and restore. And so each premarital experience must be addressed with your spouse. Once married, the experience is not just yours, but his to bear with you. As Paul said, "Bear one another's burdens." Your wounds are now his, and his wounds yours. Your individual losses affect each other and your experience in sex. Yet there is great joy in a love that overcomes. What a wonder it is to be welcomed in love, to not be alone with your losses but to be with another who loves in spite of the loss. Love does cover a multitude of sins. God delights to redeem and rescue, and He's at work in this aspect of your marriage, too.

You see, it's not just our individual mistakes that come with us to marriage. Lurking below the surface for every husband and every wife, in every marriage, is our universal shame. Every one of us is imperfect and bears the stain of shame before God. If I were to ask you if you feel shame today, likely you would say no. But as a cloak, it covers us even when we're unaware of it; it's why we wear clothes every day. It's why Adam and Eve hid themselves. Hiding our nakedness isn't just for warmth or fashion, but that we might not so acutely feel our shame. But it *is* there, just below the surface, and it works like an acid drip in our marriages until we recognize it and confront it. For example, in men, shame inhibits sexual interest in their wives, for they are ashamed of their pornography addiction and/or their past abuses of women. Shame also inhibits a woman from her natural design to respond to her husband; she is distressed by her failures to remain pure or by her lack of trust. Both can make her feel unworthy, which is another hint of our common guilt. Though we long for the comfort and safety we intuitively know is to be found in the oneness of sexual intimacy, our shame often gets in the way.

The consequences of sexual sin and abuse are not quickly overcome. But again, I want to say there is great hope for each of us in marriage, to know and be known as we recover that which was lost, piece by precious piece. Being transparent in a protected "till death do us part" commitment ushers in the safety and comfort we long for as we address what we've lost.

Thirty years ago, good friends of ours got married assuming all was well. Both had become strong believers in college, and today they are leading a great church. But about the time of their first anniversary, the wife went to the gynecologist for her annual checkup and discovered she had HPV and the early stages of cervical cancer. She was a virgin before marriage, and so the quest for answers began. She soon found out the truth from her husband. During his freshman year, prior to becoming a Christian, he had been sexually active. But after his day of redemption, he stopped and never had sex again until he married his wife. He had unknowingly contracted the HPV virus from one of these encounters, four years prior to their marriage. Since he had no symptoms, he was as shocked as she, and devastated . . . realizing his sin could kill his beloved wife. She underwent surgery, and he had to have warts removed. In time she was cleared of cancer cells, and in the years since, she has given birth to three sons. Her annual checkup is a constant reminder of their deliverance by grace. Theirs is now a secret garden secure for its intended purpose. But there was some serious weeding and replanting to do in the early years.

The ideal for marriage is one in which both spouses are true virgins, unstained by any sexual experience, abuse, or pornography, but this is rare. Yet even the purest of relationships necessitate adjustments to each other's expectations, comfort levels, and personality preferences. What one spouse feels comfortable with, the other may not. Even in the absence of emotional damage, sin still raises its ugly head in bouts of selfishness, pride, high control, manipulation, and demanding one's own way. Couples can disagree about multitudes of everyday experiences, but sexual disagreements can be like no other.

Past sexual experiences, our universal shame, and all our miscellaneous baggage make the work of creating a beautiful secret garden more complicated than it was intended. Yet gratefully, with much love comes much forgiveness (see Luke 7:47).

It is in exposure to each other that we find the healing love intends for us. This is the glorious beauty of marriage: that two injured, imperfect, sinful souls can live together in harmony and thereby demonstrate to the world that the intentions of God's original beautiful redemptive design are possible. Every marriage that not only survives but thrives fearlessly in spite of all obstacles is building a sweet victory garden of great pleasure and joy.

One of my favorite phrases in the Bible speaks to all of us, broken trees that we are, damaged, infected, or unhealthy. "And such were some of you" (1 Corinthians 6:11). This verse tells of a change, a shift, a rebirth. Past tense is no more. It is a new day. Hope is speaking words of promise for our deliverance from sin to freedom and beauty. None who enter the garden through the gates of matrimony arrive unscathed by the darkness of sin. But every one of the redeemed—you and I!—have been washed clean and set apart for His purposes and His plans, as individuals and in our marriages. We are building this secret garden in the midst of ruin, but with hope, always with hope.

- Be brave and risk sharing pieces of your story, one by one, with your beloved so that healing can begin in your secret garden.

- God loves to redeem. It's His greatest joy.

- Nothing is too hard for Him. Even this.

- Be courageous and keep working on your secret garden even when it seems impossible.

May your gardening be filled with that hope, because He is able to do exceedingly beyond all we ask or think.

Mom

Desert Gardening

Mom,

Your last letter gave me such a good overall perspective and helped me understand why sex is so complicated. But I have a friend, actually more than one, who is desperate because her husband isn't interested in sex with her. At least not like she imagined. I'm going to give her a copy of your last letter, but she feels hopeless. What do I say to her?

My dearest girls,

I'm glad you asked, because this is a sad new reality for many new brides, who are shocked to discover prince charming is ambivalent about sex. Creating a secret garden feels impossible for these young women because they don't even know what is wrong.

Most likely your friend's problem is related to some previous sexual experience in her husband's youth, like pornography or sexual abuse, so this letter will be a dive into deep waters. I have read numerous articles and books and listened to enough *FamilyLife Today* radio guests to know that the ripple effects in our culture from sexual exposures, whether mild or severe, are crippling to their victims. Pornography is devastating to young men, especially those who were exposed as little boys. In their shame, anger, and confusion most keep their past abuse a secret. Many assume that one day in marriage the temptation to view pornography will be gone, but it is an addiction not easily overcome.

Because your friend and many like her are both devastated and confused, they need advice from those who have been there and from experts. To help me answer your question and those questions your friend didn't verbalize, I've asked several young women who experienced the same situation for the lessons they learned. I also asked several of our friends who are trained therapists. This is a serious problem, and the devil of hell is delighting in all the lives and marriages he is ruining. The destruction he is causing makes me angry. In this letter is not just sound advice but also a prayer for this generation of wives to be bold, courageous, and brave believers in the hope of Christ instead of acquiescing to the lure of the culture to just find another man.

First from my young friends. One began her advice by saying, "Be careful and guard your heart, for you are very vulnerable to the affections of another man, even if you feel that is impossible right now. Don't be friends with other men on Facebook, don't have conversations during your small group with another husband without one of your spouses being present. Simply don't be friends with other men." She said, "Assume you are weak, because you are without the affection and attention you desire from your husband. Though your husband may not understand your loss, you are being neglected in your marriage, and as a result, the interest of another man might be the spark beginning a fire that destroys your marriage."

Her advice is very wise. And it has application to marriages that are not in this vulnerable place. All marriages are in the bull's-eye of the enemy of our souls, Satan himself; marriage lived well is a reflection of the Trinity, which Satan hates. Therefore, no one is exempt from his angry attacks. I believe it would be a mistaken assumption to think otherwise. When we remodeled our house, there were many days when I spent more time with our builder than I did with my husband. I work with men in our ministry, too, and can spend hours some days with men other than my husband, but I am always aware and "on guard," knowing I am not beyond falling. I don't live in fear, but I live with a healthy fear of God, knowing that He sees all and that it is Him I want to please.

Another young friend said this about our letter topic: "Quit trying to fix him, win him, and change him. And don't assume it's all your fault, either. Too often we women in this circumstance think, *If I do this sexual act he will find me attractive*, but something is broken deep inside him that your actions can't heal. Your responsibility is to respect him and love him well and encourage him to find help."

My sweet friend continued her story, telling me for the first two or three years of her marriage she kept her anguish to herself and pretended all was well. She tried everything she could think of to make herself attractive to her new husband, assuming she must be doing something wrong. Nothing worked. Finally, she could keep quiet no more and began talking to her friends and family about how awful life was for her. In hindsight she realized this was a huge mistake, because in telling her story she had exposed her husband's weakness and flaws to others who would now always see him this way. Finally, they began counseling, and at year five in their marriage she began to have hope.

Our dear friend Dan Allender is a therapist and author of many books, several of which specialize in sexual abuse and trauma. In response to an email I sent him with this question, he replied with insight gained from years and years of listening to deep heartbreak and unspeakable travesty forced upon children around the world. It is the strength and love of Christ that can sustain a man who has borne a burden this heavy, and it is the wisdom of God that Dan shared with me and I now pass on to you.

Mistakenly, we think pornography is about sex, that men seek it out because they aren't satisfied at home, or we assume it's about lust or an insatiable appetite. Dan says this is the lie. It is not just about sex. And there might be some relief for your friend to know that pornography is *not* about her. It isn't even about the fact that he has struggled with it since he was eight or ten or twelve. The real heart issue, Dan says, is the man's desire to make someone pay for all the hurt, heartache, failure, and rejection he has felt over his lifetime. No, he is not thinking of you when he views pornography. The unnamed women on the screen or wherever he goes are the surrogates for his anger. But still, you pay, because after his heartache or anger or rage is spent, you live with the man full of apathy and shame who returns to you a shell.

Yes, men are pulled into viewing pornography by the temptation to lust. Every man carries that weakness, that brokenness, which feels satisfied when he looks at naked women. Every man struggles with lust, even those who regularly win the battle. But men who are addicted to pornography by choice or by childhood abuse have added anger and victim issues that complicate what is for unharmed men more simply a struggle to control their thought life.

What are your friend and the thousands of young wives like her to do? Dan gave me four suggestions that I want to pass on to you.

First, Dan says, "Give up the assumption that it is your fault" and that therefore you must change. Just as my young friend said, "Quit trying to fix it yourself."

Second,

> Try to understand more deeply the sense of frustration and futility he feels as a consequence of Adam and Eve's fall. He feels fury and is easily entitled, angry, distant, and defeated as he faces the daily thorns and thistles that block the ease of making life work. All men feel the pull of lust. But men addicted to pornography are driven there by more than lust. The addicted man is drawn to pornography as it allows him satisfaction without risk and revenge without consequences. It is an issue of rage and cowardice combined to create a commitment to degrade a woman sexually.

I will add that all men need the safety only their wives can provide. At home in your secret garden—and I don't mean in the act of sex, but in your bedroom or any private place you share—the comfort that comes from knowing one other person understands, cares, and is helping to bear the heavy burdens of life gives courage and strength to get up and face another day. Your husband needs your support and respect and belief to conquer this challenge or any other. God made us to need one another.

Third,

> When pornography is found on a computer or in a drawer, don't accept an apology or a commitment to change. The problem is already a cancer. What is required is accountability and wisdom. Accountability can come when enough men in his life know of the problem to be a force of goodness in prayer, direct interaction, and confession. No one addresses this problem

alone with success. Wisdom grows when the deeper roots of anger are seen in the struggle itself.

A good therapist or pastoral counselor is necessary, as my young friends have experienced. Both of my friends I quoted above would say having a skilled biblical listener was invaluable.

Last, Dan said that in these marriages, it is not just the work a husband must do; this is a journey for both of you. No one is unscathed or unstained by sexual sin and abuse, as I said in my last letter. Both of you can move toward sexual wholeness and holiness, sharing not only the pain of such work but also the joy of restoration and victory over the darkness the father of lies so eagerly sows for our destruction. Sexual sin in this broken world is sadly inevitable, but it is not, as Dan said, "the final word." What hope that gives, just to read that phrase, "Not the final word." I rejoice in this greater truth and feel hopeful for your friend, if there is willingness to enter the battle necessary to accomplish victory.

It is only when we throw ourselves at God's mercy and abandon all escape routes that He can and will make Himself known.

In the end, it is forgiveness that brings the miracle of redemption—not a forgiveness that ignores the sin, but one that comes from entering the darkness with your man, confident that God will redeem your great risk to believe. I have said it before and perhaps I should close every letter with these words, but here it is especially necessary. "With men it is impossible, but not with God; for with God all things are possible" (Mark 10:27 NKJV). The impossibility of living with the heartache and loss from a pornography addiction has led many women to leave their husband for another man. Just this fall I heard of another young woman, a believing woman with two small children, who gave up after living with this seemingly impossible situation for ten years. But I pray that for your friend and many other courageous young women, there will be the hope of a complete abandonment to the greater truth that all things are possible with God. It is only when we throw ourselves at His mercy and abandon all escape routes that He can and will make Himself known.

Any man, unless there are medical reasons, can grow to become a better lover. He can face the wounds of his past and rise above the ashes. He was made to sacrifice himself in love as Christ did for us. He can learn to initiate sex. And initiating lovemaking is one way he can learn to set aside passivity and step up to a greater level of manhood. But only after doing the necessary work of restoration and renewal.

Remember:

- A pornography addiction is not the wife's fault.

- A trained therapist or pastoral counselor is needed.

- "With God all things are possible." Dare to believe Him.

I pray that many young women in your generation will be warriors for righteousness in their marriages, strong with the weapons of prayer and faith, defenders of God's vision for their secret garden.

Believing the impossible with you,
Mom

Pulling Weeds, Planting Seeds

Dear Mom,

We've come so far on the sex front. But there are lingering issues that keep cropping up, rearing their ugly little heads. They seem to plague us and pull us away from all that this aspect of our marriage is supposed to be like. And I basically thought this was all going to get easier with time. Now that the kids are older . . . I just thought we'd be past all this and onto something better. And frankly, there's a part of me that just wants to shelve this aspect of our life altogether. Isn't hand holding and cuddling enough? Really?

Dear daughters,

An important task in our annual yard work responsibilities is covering our beds and borders with a layer of pine-straw mulch. Working like a blanket, mulch suppresses weed growth—I didn't say eliminates—and it reduces water evaporation by protecting the soil from extreme temperatures. Safeguarding our investment is worth the annual work to rake and clean all the planted areas and then to haul and spread the mulch. Sometimes we try to get by with less to save money and time, but we always regret it when we watch thousands of weeds sprouting through the mulch.

It is abundantly clear that no secret garden blooms without steady, attentive work. But unlike rebuilding the physical walls of a garden—which can be reconstructed in one season—gardening in marriage requires a longer view, a vision of what can be, in time. Often your dad and I felt the truth of "One step forward, two steps back," for it is, as Mike Mason says in *The Mystery of Marriage*, "the special work of sin to destroy trust and intimacy, to bring about enmity and alienation between people." Our culture is saturated with sex, but it's a skewed, warped saturation, which makes building a healthy sexual relationship—as God created and intended it to be—all the more difficult.

Another necessary task for growth in gardening is amending the soil. It must be dug up and turned to loosen the hard places, with soil conditioners added for enriching. Interestingly, some of the best fertilizers are manures, the refuse of the animal world; this parallels the breaking down of sin in our lives, which ultimately produces the sweet fruits of compassion, greater love, more patience, and gentle kindness. Gardening and marriage require attention to remain healthy. A secret garden cannot be neglected.

But maintenance is dirty work. There is a scientific truth, the second law of thermodynamics, that says everything in the universe is moving from order to disorder, from life to death. Everywhere it is seen: in astronomy, where stars like our sun gradually cool; in the tiny world of microbes, where mini-creatures constantly eat away at other dead or dying organisms; and in our realm of existence, where everything naturally falls apart: your car, your yard, your house, neighborhood streets, downtown buildings, and entire city systems. And of course, disorder happens naturally in gardens.

If marriage is the most important human relationship, why would we expect our marriage relationships to be exempt from the downward pull of decay? There are no exceptions to this law.

During the first year of our marriage, Dennis led a Bible study for men, which met at our house. In the presence of one of the men, I began to feel uncomfortable. He seemed too friendly. But was I just imagining things? Perhaps I was paranoid. He was married and so was I. But after a few of these sessions, I decided to share how I felt with my husband. It wasn't easy. I feared Dennis would think I was inviting this man's attention. Or might he assume I had a suspicious mind? Was I believing the worst?

I took the risk, we talked, and your dad moved the Bible study to a restaurant. Problem solved. But we both learned a very valuable lesson: the importance of facing things together and not becoming isolated.

This is accountability at its best, where it matters most, in our marriages. If we keep our temptations or our fears secretly within—thinking *I can handle this, he/she doesn't need to know*—we will become vulnerable to lots of weed growth. Woody weeds can grow strong enough to crack concrete, so beware of minimizing these threats to your garden. In hindsight, your dad and I both believe this situation was the enemy trying to derail our young marriage.

Years later, after all six of you kids had arrived and I was tired all the time, your dad began to share with me when he, too, faced temptation, an attraction to another woman, usually due to the fact that he and I had not made enough time for intimacy. There were times when I felt upon hearing his struggle that I was failing. I knew the problem wasn't the other woman, but his need for me. My first response was to say I was sorry, which was true. I didn't want him to face those kinds of unwanted distractions. Then we talked about how we could be together more often to eliminate this temptation. Because I felt compassion for him, I wanted to help protect him, not to leave him weak and vulnerable. My heart's desire was and is to be an available wife, attentive and caring as much as I can be. There is a sense of duty here that is not wrong. I cannot insist on my own way and my own timing without consequences for him. "Bear one another's burdens" is not just for the church. If my husband is feeling a burden of temptation, it is his job to stand against it, and my job to do all I can to help him stand strong. Why? Because I have to? No, because I love him, and I do not want him leaving home vulnerable and weak.

Your most important accountability partner is your husband, not someone else. And being accountable in marriage is not for accusations. A formal meeting is not needed for this, but rather a freedom to risk being transparent, knowing your spouse will respond well, with time, and with love. There will never be freedom to share struggles and temptations if there is fear of ridicule or judgment. You must invite each other to the safety of a marital relationship that never fears exposure outside your walls. Like a soft, deep layer of mulch, transparency in your marriage will keep most weed seeds dormant and unable to sprout.

The bottom line is, don't let isolation in. Don't let pride or fear keep you from sharing your thoughts with each other. Many of our men feel they must always be strong, but a wise woman knows her husband has fears and insecurities that she can nurse and strengthen privately in their own garden sanctuary. Pull those weeds regularly.

Now for the rest of the story.

There are landscape features in our secret garden that are known only to us and to the Father. Places that together with Him we have rebuilt, replanted, and nurtured into bloom again. Years of seasons have come and gone in our garden. Many seasons of springtime beauty and many winters of apparent barrenness have cycled in and out of our marriage, yet in those days of cold, we knew with patience spring would come again.

Like a soft,
deep layer of mulch,

transparency

IN YOUR MARRIAGE

will keep most
weed seeds dormant
and unable to sprout.

In the last years of our parenting journey, when our youngest were finishing high school, we talked often about the future. What would our relationship be like? What would sex be like? It was winter again. I was a very weary woman in those years, and my interest in my husband was primarily one of responsibility and not eager engagement. But I had hope that when the burden of daily mothering was over that the real me would emerge again, almost like a rebirth. Neither of us knew if we could recapture our once-upon-a-time first love, but we hoped. We hoped for spring.

And now it has come again. Not the same kind of spring, of course, but a richer, deeper blooming, full of appreciation and wonder for the Creator of it all. Like comparing kindergarten art with a Rembrandt or a Sargent, or a bean plant in a paper cup with the gardens of Versailles outside Paris or Butchart Gardens in Canada—we would never trade today's secret garden for yesterday's. Numberless lessons have been learned over the decades of our union. Countless books have been read. Forgiveness has been asked for and granted seventy times seventy. And counseling sessions have added to our growth as gardeners of our secret place, like workshops and continuing education do in any other field. Yes, it is work. Don't be deceived into thinking otherwise. But it has been a worthy investment, a worthy effort with beautiful satisfying results.

- You have to be willing to get dirty, to see and touch the mud, to coax new life to grow.

- Weeding is ongoing. It will never be finished.

- Remember in the winters of your marriage that spring can come again if you don't give up.

May it be so for you, and may your marriage be a display of God's glory for your generation.

With great love for each of you,
Mom

P.S. Here's another issue in today's world that can directly affect the satisfaction of a couple's sexual relationship. It may not be your situation but it may be a friend's. Because so many women work full-time and have significant careers, marriages can experience unique challenges previous generations never faced. It's a new day for men and women. Many couples today are trying new roles, where dad stays home with the kids while mom works. We don't have long-term data to know yet how those marriages work for a lifetime or if the children fare as well with a stay-at-home dad. Your dad and I have known couples who early on seemed to manage well their reversed roles, but over time the marriage became strained. One couple we knew well divorced after about twelve years of her being the sole provider and him the stay-at-home parent. She told us, "He wasn't leading the family."

Women in this situation who make a "claim to godliness" (1 Timothy 2:10 NASB), who care about pleasing God, must be brave enough to ask some hard questions: *Does my husband feel undermined by my successful career? How does he really feel about my greater earning power? Is he fully able to develop his gifts by staying home with the children? Is he becoming all God designed him to be in this arrangement we are testing?* If he begins to feel insignificant or less important as a man, will you be courageous enough to consider denying yourself your career for his good and the health of your marriage and family? Are you watching and listening closely? Are you willing to follow God's lead regardless?

It is clear in the Bible that God gifted women to be nurturers. Men do not have that DNA strength. So as women, we must believe God's design enough to yield to it if Dad's staying home full-time isn't working as you had both hoped.

When a healthy, able-bodied man feels needed, when he feels primary responsibility to protect his wife and children and to provide financially, he usually steps up to that assignment. Sometimes that's just not an option for a couple—like for Ian and Larissa Murphy, whose future was forever changed when Ian suffered a traumatic brain injury as they were preparing to marry. Four years later they married, and now tell a remarkable story of marital love and faith in their book, *Eight Twenty Eight* (B&H Books, 2014). How does Larissa make her disabled husband feel respected and needed? It takes extra effort and energy—which I know many working women feel is in short supply, but it's important to figure it out. There aren't easy answers, but a determination to do marriage by the Creator's plan is the best answer to these modern dilemmas. God will show you how if He's called you to be an exception, as He has called Larissa. And after watching their story, I doubt her exception is what most women had in mind. (Learn more about Ian and Larissa's story at ianandlarissa.com.)

May the Lord bless you and keep you and give you the eyes of faith to continue to believe that He who called you to this man of yours will give you all that you need to make it not only work but become a display of great beauty.

GROWING ROSES

After reading *The Secret Garden* and watching the movie several times, I began to imagine creating our own secret garden here on our sunset ridge lane. I envisioned pathways and blooming plants . . . but especially roses. Roses are the most popular of garden plants because of their beauty and their fragrance. And they are perennial, which means they bloom all summer, year after year after year. But there are two significant detractions—roses are susceptible to black spot, a disease that will eventually kill them, and they have thorns. To my knowledge, no one has produced a thornless rose. Some have fewer or smaller thorns, but a truly thornless variety has not yet been cultivated.

Several months ago, Dennis and I had another thorny conversation about sex. But instead of getting stuck by the same things we'd said dozens of times before, with no resolution, this time he asked a question he'd never thought to ask before. He asked if I would explain what I meant when I said, "I sometimes feel confused about our sex life." He showed genuine interest when he said, "I'd like to hear more about what you mean." I hadn't really thought about what I meant in depth, and since we were driving to visit a friend in another town, we had time for an uninterrupted conversation. And the result was greater understanding than we'd had before. We heard each other at a deeper level. The Lord stripped away those particular thorns.

Long ago, inside our gold wedding bands, we inscribed two verses: Genesis 2:25, "And the man and his wife were both naked and were not ashamed," was in one, and in the other, 1 John 4:18, "Perfect love casts out fear." Though we were both incredibly naïve at the time, we knew enough to recognize that we both were bringing fears into our marriage. Fears of rejection, fears of what the future would hold, fears of inadequacy, fears of failure, and hundreds more. In fact, a good friend suggested during our engagement that we each write down all our fears about marriage, talk about them together, and then commit them to Christ, which we did. It was good and healthy, but it just scratched the surface. You see, fear is a permanent scar from the fall. All of us carry its mark; some just hide and mask it better than others. If Adam and Eve hid from God—who is the epitome of perfect love, grace, and mercy—of course we will hide even more carefully from anyone else who we perceive can hurt us.

What your dad and I discovered again that day in the car was that fear was still lurking and we were unaware. But once we brought it into the light, it was exposed, its power was gone. "If we walk in the light, as he is in the light, we have fellowship with one another, and the blood of Jesus his Son cleanses us from all sin" (1 John 1:7).

It is easier to mask our fears publically than privately. We want to appear to have it all together, to be on top of life, to come across as if we need nothing. But the truth is we are desperately needy, and in marriage we can hopefully find the safety to be vulnerable about those needs. Dare to go there with your man.

The most beautiful long-stemmed roses also have the largest thorns. We just don't see them very often, because some florist created a genius

little tool that strips them off the stems. The roses in your secret garden can be de-thorned, too—through years of tender, devoted love and attention.

- Face your fears and keep exposing them to the light.

- It's okay that you will never achieve perfection (we won't, either).

- But a great deal of safety and security, lost in Eden, can be found again in the secret garden of marriage.

Keep enriching the soil of your marriage so that you can grow never-before-seen beauties of grace.

Mom

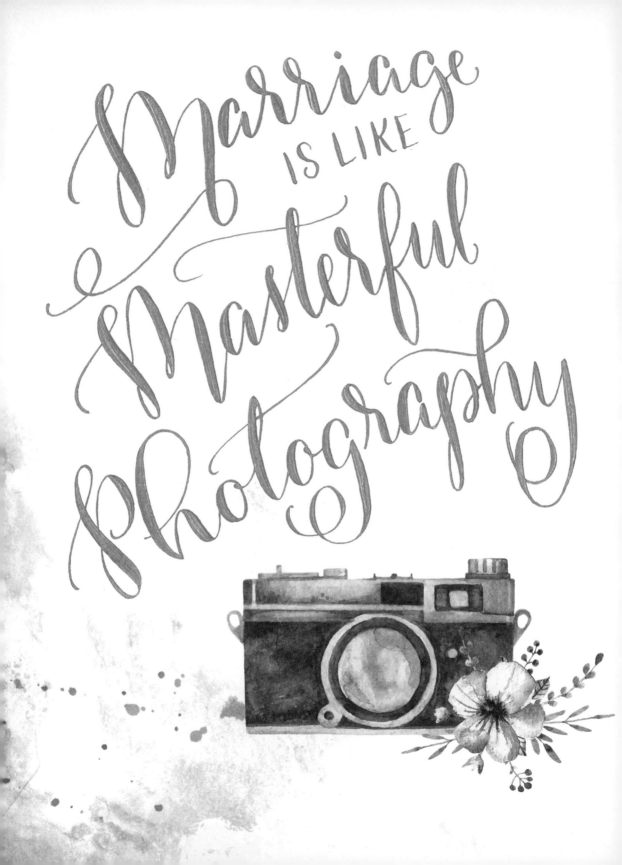

Marriage
IS LIKE
Masterful
Photography

A few years ago, two of our family photographers, Ashley and Stephanie, set aside some time to take photos of Ashley's two boys, one a toddler and one just learning to crawl. Stephanie and Ashley set up a black background, which hid everything in the living room that would detract from seeing baby James. The black background also highlighted the purity of his little body with his soft, clear baby skin. Our favorite photo of James shows him playfully on his hands and knees, looking to the side with a precious grin on his face.

When taking the picture of James, Stephanie made a decision to focus her camera on his sweet face, making sure the light illuminated his most important features. By contrast, she and Ashley could have chosen to put James in the backyard in the mud and then irritated him so that they could capture his mad face on film forever. Instead, they believed what was worth remembering was the innocence in his face, the beautiful potential of a baby's earliest months of life.

Everyone with a camera in his or her hand makes a decision of focus, a choice to capture a memorable moment or event in hopes it will not be forgotten. Beauty often inspires a shutter click, for behind every camera lens someone believes this slice of a vista, this moment of time, is worth remembering. Saying yes to the one means you say no to much more.

Professional photographers embedded with troops on the battlefield, for instance, make decisions to exclude scenes or images that would be objectionable, offensive, or counterproductive to the war effort. Photographers have control. And so do you. Like them, you make hundreds of decisions a day with the lens of your heart, to show what you want others to see about your husband and your marriage. Photography is a creative form of communication, of telling a story, of sending an important message. So, too, are words.

The story of your marriage is yours to frame and develop.

What I believe about Dennis is the starting place for everything I say or don't say. We wives choose what others will see in our husbands by what we focus on when we talk about him. What you believe is what will grow. What you see is what others will see. The story of your marriage is yours to frame and develop.

Learning to Focus

Hey, Mom,

Sometimes I get tired of being discouraged by all the unexpected things I have to deal with that come from the way my husband lives life. It's not just that we are different—you already wrote me about that. It's more than that. It's like I think if I didn't have him, sometimes life would be easier. It is kind of nice when he is out of town for a few days. But I am glad when he comes back, too. I don't know. Maybe you felt this way about the laundry situation you faced, but mine feels harder to me. I just don't know what to do about it all. Does that make any sense at all?

My daughter,

Do you remember how alert and energized you were when you were dating? I do. It was like you'd had a double espresso every hour of the day! Wonder at being noticed, chosen, and then loved inspired creative dates, conversations, and dreams. Inspiration is a capacity bestowed on us by God and makes us like Him. Because you were often delighted by new revelations in this man of yours, it was easy to speak of him in glowing terms to anyone who would listen. You were creating word pictures, photographs of what you saw in him. Your storytelling had begun. But sometimes stories drag and lose their punch. Storytellers know they have to go back to the big idea to refocus their words in order to keep the audience engaged; likewise, your marriage story needs periodic adjustments in focus, too.

All photographers begin with an experience, a vision, or a stirring that then leads to a decision of focus. A beautiful scene, a stunning moment, or a passing milestone shouts to be remembered forever. Likewise, beauty in a relationship calls us to capture what our eyes behold. By contrast, disappointment in a relationship clouds our vision and saps our energy so that even the beauty of nature goes unnoticed.

Over the years of our marriage, Dennis has said repeatedly that one of the best gifts I've ever given him is my belief in him. It has always surprised me that it is that important to him, because I see him as competent and strong. But the truth is he, like all men, has an underlying need to be bolstered by the loyal, confident belief of the most important person in his life. Me. As I wrote in a previous letter, our men need to be reminded often that we will be with them forever, just as God says throughout the Bible to different people in every circumstance: "I will be with you; I will not leave you." Our men need to hear words of support and encouragement. Belief is simply the choice to focus on what is good and true and yes, lovely. It's cheering him on, helping him believe what you see and know to be true, just as God does for us.

Men wonder if they can really do all that is expected of them. In their moments of doubt, sometimes more frequent than we women would imagine, in the darkroom of their souls they are asking, *Can I do this? Can I develop this image of manhood God expects of me, that my wife expects of me, that my children need from me? I don't know if I have what it takes to become a godly man, a husband, a father, a provider, a sacrificial leader, and a servant. And is my job secure? Am I doing enough?*

He is oh so aware of his inadequacy for any one of these responsibilities, and for the unknowns that lie ahead in this call of God to love and lead his family as Christ does the church. It can be paralyzing. The lure to selfishness, immaturity, and adolescence, the easy road, is never far away, whereas the call to responsibility and maturity is the steep, rocky path.

Sometimes it is helpful in photography to step back and look at your subject from a different vantage point before you decide on the best composition. Taking the shot from the side or above creates a unique perspective that may be more interesting than a straightforward, perfectly centered focus. Let's climb a ladder for a different view of your man.

From what you know of the Bible, how does God see you? Does He know you are flawed? Yes. Does He see only your broken places? No. How does He describe you? He sees you as the apple of His eye, adopted, as His child, holy and blameless in Christ, a royal heir, and forgiven; always and forever, He sees you and me as forgiven. In the midst of some of our darkest days when I *felt* very little love for my man, these lenses of faith kept the glimmer of

> Love convinces a couple that they are the greatest romance that has ever been, that no two people have ever loved as they do, and that they will sacrifice absolutely anything in order to be together. And then marriage asks them to prove it.
>
> —Mike Mason, *The Mystery of Marriage*

hope alive. I never stopped believing in a God who can do the impossible, which meant my husband was not impossible, I was not impossible, nor was our situation impossible to God.

Part of my calling and privilege as a wife is to believe that all of this and more is true about my husband, and to help him believe it, too. So when we have conversations about our failures and disappointments, it is always in the context of belief in each other, in the truth of the gospel that we are and can be overcomers. Once I cease to see the reality of what God can do in my husband's life, then he senses that lack of support and confidence. With our lens focused on all that is wrong, we communicate disdain or displeasure or disappointment. Yes, you feel disappointment, and it's okay that you do. And yes, you need to communicate your hurt or your sadness, but not at the expense of his worth. Express how his actions made you feel instead of framing the conversation or debate in accusatory *you* statements. Instead of saying, "You are so insensitive," which is a way of labeling him as always insensitive, instead say, "When you make comments or observations like that, I feel you aren't considering how hard I've worked all day." So speak about how you feel, but don't use words or statements that portray him as a failure, inadequate, or hopeless.

Often I have had to confess to God that I'm only seeing what I don't like. When I recognize my selfish focus on what I want or wish, then I ask God to change my heart. Cataracts form in every eye if you live long enough, but their removal restores clear vision. So repentance in my heart restores joy and the capacity to see beauty once again. As long as we remain proud, clinging to what we think we deserve, we will be blind, unable to marvel at anything lovely in our relationship or in our husband.

In 1 Corinthians 13 one of the phrases says, "Love believes all things," which doesn't mean love believes *everything*. There is much spoken and written that is false, so the call is to believe what is true. Therefore, love always believes because truth will triumph. In my marriage my goal is to always believe the best about my husband, to always believe God is not finished with him yet, and to always believe the best is yet to come. It's finding and focusing on the positive by faith. And if in the moment you can't see a single trait worthy of praising, then cling to the truth of how God sees him and you. Ask God, as I have done many, many times, to help you see your husband as God Himself sees him.

Remember, he married you because he felt bolstered by your love, by your belief that he was the coolest, the most handsome, the most sensitive, the most (fill in the blank) of any man you had ever dated. He felt he could conquer the world with you at his side. Keep giving him that belief, and God will reward.

- Focus is a decision of what to include in the frame and how to keep disappointments in proper perspective.

- Confess, repent, and believe again when you focus on faults.

- Believing in your man is a great gift only you can give.

Always,
Mom

Photoshop and Filters

Mom,

All the women in my small group went to a fondue place for dinner last week. It was so great to get out without husbands and kids for once, but I was a little uncomfortable when a couple of the women started talking about their husbands' faults. I certainly agreed. Mine does the same things, too, but I just didn't know what to say. We all felt kinda awkward for a while.

Dear daughters,

Somewhere around our tenth or twelfth year of marriage, we were in a small group at church with some other couples. I don't remember the composition of the group anymore, except for one couple. They were a bit older than we and lived in an older expensive neighborhood that oozed status to me. He was a successful businessman, but it is the wife I remember so very well because she frequently made little negative comments about her husband as we mingled in groups before or after our study. She never raised her voice. She remained calm and even elegant in her demeanor, but the air turned to ice for a second or two before someone else spoke into the chill.

Like you, I always felt uncomfortable and wanted to escape to another conversation. Even worse, at times she made little jabs when he could hear. I felt bad for him. Gossip is as destructive as a leaky ceiling, but when it's a wife undermining her husband publically with her words, it can be deadly. Our group changed at the end of that year and we didn't see this couple as regularly, but I wasn't surprised to learn several years later that they were divorced.

Solomon said, "There is nothing new under the sun" (Ecclesiastes 1:9), and he is right, for women have struggled with complaining about their men for centuries. While there is a level of naïveté with many women, I don't buy ignorance as the only reason wives often say too much. We are intuitive, and we know it's not right. But in the moment we can forget that once a word is spoken it cannot be retrieved. Even worse is the danger of social media, for those messages are burned onto hard drives.

With our voices we communicate a picture of our husbands; words make an impression, an image in the imagination as lasting as a photograph. With our words we can inspire others with what inspired us.

Like everyone in America, I'm sure you remember exactly where you were and what you were doing on the morning of September 11, 2001. One of the stories from that fateful day was of Todd Beamer, who with a few other brave men rushed the cockpit of flight 93, hoping to wrest the plane from the hijackers and keep it from its intended destruction in Washington, D.C. In doing so they perished.

Within hours, Lisa Beamer was thrust into the public spotlight. The whole nation wanted to know about the young husband and father who said, "Let's roll," signaling the men to move forward to their deaths. Lisa only knew what the rest of the nation knew about those last moments of his life, but she knew a lot more about the man Todd had become. In countless interviews she had the opportunity to reveal an image of her husband as she chose words to describe what he was like. In doing so, she developed photographs in our minds.

What Lisa teaches us is that wives have similar opportunities, though not as public, to build their husband's reputation by what they say to others. Lisa focused naturally on the best qualities in her husband as she remembered his life. His death made that easier for her to do than for those of us who are reminded on a daily basis of our living husband's imperfections. His death crystallized in an instant what was truly important about Todd.

Building your husband's reputation might at times feel impossible,

Wives have opportunities to build their husband's reputation by what they say to others because you know the real truth about his flaws as no one else does. It's very hard at times not to focus on the ugly, especially for those of us who are perfectionists and who have high standards.

One of the statements I always make when I speak at the Weekend to Remember is, "Never criticize your husband in public," and I usually add, "or at home in front of your children." Why? Because I believe that much of what people think about my husband is based on my opinion. If I communicate that I don't trust him, why would anyone else trust him? If I complain to others about his faults, what will others see when they are around him? They will see him as I've portrayed him.

In spite of the abuse directed toward the woman in Proverbs 31 over the last several decades, it is supremely instructive that the first of her accolades is about her marriage. Before all the super-woman activities are listed comes this statement: "The heart of her husband trusts in her" (v. 11). One of the greatest needs of every man is a wife he can trust implicitly. He doesn't have to wonder what she asked her small group to pray for about him. Anxiety doesn't walk in the door when you walk out to go visit your mother or spend the afternoon with your sister. When you are with groups of friends in your neighborhood or church, he isn't feeling his stomach turn wondering if his wife will say something that is embarrassing.

We place a high value on freedom of speech and being oneself in our culture. Both are worthy qualities. It is also good that women have found their voice. This progress was needed. But when we try to learn a new skill, we often make lots of mistakes in the process. In our greater freedom to speak we have lost the virtue of restraint. Self-control does not mean ignoring what is real in relationships. It refers to managing impulses, the selfish desire to lash out, to spray a volley of hurtful words at someone just to show how badly they hurt you, or to a friend to show how badly your husband hurt you, how uncaring he is. Brutal honesty without regard to how it will affect another is insensitive to both the third party and most importantly to your husband.

The opportunities you have to build your husband's reputation are actually more important than Lisa's because Todd Beamer's life is finished. His work is done. Lisa is summarizing his life when she talks about Todd.

But your husband's work on this planet is not finished. Neither is yours. You have great power to influence not just his reputation but the man he will become by the words you choose. Will you enhance his image when you talk to others about him? Will you find the beautiful and good as you photoshop his image? Or will you expose his faults, which are still very alive, even by way of a lighthearted joke? Words are powerful.

Just to be clear, photoshopping in this analogy is not lying. It's not faking it or creating a false image. Instead, it's placing the very real person your husband is in the best possible light. All photographers use real people. Only cartoonists create caricatures.

There is wisdom in the phrase "Let every person be quick to hear, slow to speak" (James 1:19). When it comes to talking about your husband to others, wisdom knows that once words are spoken they cannot be retrieved. Another piece of wisdom came from Thumper, in the movie *Bambi*, who when reproved repeated his father's words, "If you can't say something nice, don't say anything at all." Works for children and for adults.

- Grade your verbal self-control, your self-restraint. Do you score an A, a C, or a failing grade?

- Does the heart of your husband trust you? Are you willing to ask him?

- What kinds of images are you creating, beautiful or ugly?

- Remember, *you* control what others know about your man.

Love,
Mom

P.S. So how do you help your family know and love this man you married? What then can you say to your family about your husband? What can you tell your mother or father, sisters and brothers? Your parents have spent their whole lives loving you and protecting you and wanting the best for you. Remember, it will be difficult for them to hear you are suffering or lonely or angry or disappointed. It will make it harder for them to love your husband if they know he is failing you in some way. Your parents may want to continue to love your young husband, but they could find it difficult to resist the temptation to become critical or withdraw. Though nothing may ever be said, your husband may sense something has changed, and he may feel rejected and unworthy. Remember, he is not stupid.

It might help to remember that your own family might initially feel a greater emotional loyalty to you because they've known and loved you longer. Your spouse is the newcomer in your family. He is not loved less, just known less. You and your parents have history together, as does he with his family. So if you share a disappointment with your sister, she will probably take your side and be tempted to think poorly of your husband. Do you want that mistake he made to stay there and fester? You and he may solve the problem in a few days, but your sister may continue to view your husband disapprovingly for hurting you, not knowing that you have moved on. Your friends may not always be your friends for lots of reasons, but your family will always be your family. Photoshop well what your family views in your husband. Inspire their love by the images you share.

LEARNING TO BE HONEST
Using Transparencies and Negatives

Recently my son Samuel sent me a link to a Library of Congress collection of newly restored color photographs taken by Sergei Prokudin-Gorskii, photographer to the last tsar of Russia, Nicholas II. Taken between the years 1905 and 1915, Sergei's photographs captured what he believed was important in his beloved country. A photograph of children sitting on a hillside on a warm summer afternoon, another of a Jewish elder teaching a group of children, and a gang of men working on the construction of a railroad trestle—all gave me glimpses into the lives of people and a culture I will never know. Each of Sergei's photographs froze one brief moment of a life forever on a transparent glass plate. In the right hands these one-hundred-year-old negatives were transformed into images of wonder. Looking at them with their striking clarity was like taking a voyage in a time machine. They were truly mesmerizing.

Everyone claims to want transparency in marriage. Our souls long to know and be known, to see and be seen, and then to be safe and at peace. But as I wrote in the letters on sex, this process of revealing the photographs of our lives is extremely complex, delicate work. In handling the one-hundred-year-old glass plates, skilled experts carefully touched only the edges of the fragile glass and coaxed images of beauty from those negatives. So in marriage, we must learn to appreciate that we are both in need of tender care for transparent beauty to emerge.

In photography, negatives are the final image in reverse. It's the glass plate or the thin film on which the image was burned by the light allowed into the lens of the camera. Without the wash of chemicals, a photographic negative shows the lightest lights as the darkest darks. And in an untrained, unknowing hand, Sergei's raw exposed plates could have been discarded, and the world would have missed the glory of their transformation into a positive, full-color image. Had someone not appreciated the value of these negatives, the beauty he captured would have been lost forever.

Stop and think about negatives with me. What if the final image in reverse is also true in your husband? What if those negatives that drive you crazy are really positives that God wants to transform into use, with your believing help, for His purposes? What if your inability to see the value in those negatives is keeping him from becoming the man you hope for and God intended? What if your husband is longing for the wash of your love and belief in him that might slowly transform those negatives into life-giving light?

The negative places in any man's life, or woman's, for that matter, are opportunities for God's transformative hand to work. When we as wives find those places and shamelessly expose them to the eyes and ears of friends or family, we are destroying the opportunity to see glory. The beauty God would create is lost. Not forever, because with God resurrection is always possible as long as we have breath, but lost for today and maybe for a long time.

One of the ongoing battles I face in my marriage relates to my view of negatives. I am very much like my father, a brilliant man (I didn't get those genes) who was also a firstborn and a perfectionist who was rarely wrong. Even in his nintieth year he was sharp and remembered a whole host of facts most of us couldn't remember if we'd read them yesterday. Inherited from my mechanical engineer father is my penchant for details, and with it my own propensity to want to be right. In our marriage, I am constantly noticing, it's worse now that it's just the two of us—the little things said incorrectly, placed incorrectly, or generally not done the way I would do it. What I view as mistakes are really negatives in God's hand that He waits to transform into glory. Life would be horribly boring if my husband were just like me, and I know it. Even knowing how good he is for me, I still struggle to control my selfish tendency to see negatively instead of letting God transform my view into delight.

I am learning to take this flawed DNA to God as soon as I become aware of something I've said or done. I did not enjoy that part of my dad's personality, his need to correct and instruct, and neither does my husband. Just last night I said to Dennis, "Someday in heaven I will be so glad to be rid of this weakness of mine to always see flaws and mistakes. I'm sorry." I immediately said to God in my next thought, "God, please help me see my husband as you see him. Help me love him as you do."

Love is the reason we get married, and it remains one of our greatest assets for influencing our husbands' lives. All of us who are believers are tasked with loving well. But a wife's loyal love that always believes the best about him is more valuable than the applause of thousands. Only you can give your husband the courage to welcome God's handiwork in his heart. Only you can understand and help carry the burdens of his life. Your opinion, your prayers, your voice, your encouragement, your love matter above all else.

When you love well, you bear with him as he is growing and working to overcome his weaknesses and deficiencies. Your love "covers" those weaknesses, as the chemicals wash and cover the glass negatives, allowing a transformation to occur. "Love covers a multitude of sins" also means you don't expose his negative flaws to the harsh light of others' judgments. His sins, faults, and handicaps are his to deal with, his to confess, his to make public if he chooses. Your love will help him feel confident enough to do that if he needs to. Knowing you will never leave and your love will never die will give him the safety to risk becoming God's man.

Remember, gentleness and humility are required when handling negatives and the chemicals that transform them.

- Becoming transparent is delicate work.

- Transforming negatives into beauty is God's delight.

- Love covers and provides safety.

May your words create respectful images of him for others to see.

Always,
Mom

A PICTURE IS WORTH A THOUSAND WORDS

Photography is the art of capturing beautiful or memorable images. Every photograph you take reveals what you value, what you believe is important. Marriage is the same. You and he control what others know and see and feel about the two of you. Again, you can control only your half, and yes, there are lessons here for him, too, but he isn't your responsibility. Focus on what you control, which is your own heart. Keep what is true and noble, pure and lovely, what is good and virtuous and worthy of praise in your husband in the lens of your camera.

In spite of all the disappointments and failures and mistakes we have both experienced in our marriage over the years, I have always come back to the central truth that God is not finished with my husband, or me, yet. In fact, one of the gifts of our long marriage is that we both keep changing and becoming more real and genuinely transparent. And, I hope, more like Jesus. I would have never believed we could still be growing and blooming. I wrongly assumed age only produced stagnation or status quo. But

Only you control what others see in your husband through the lens of your words.

gloriously and wonderfully we are being transformed, as Paul said, from glory to glory! Our broken places are not beyond repair in the hands of almighty God. That is a beautiful truth.

I hope you will remember there isn't a man alive who doesn't have significant negative spaces in his life, and we wives have enormous power to inflict harm on him if we choose. We know his weaknesses, his fears, his doubts, and even his physical insecurities—all of which are part of our intimate union with him. We have been trusted with such intimate knowledge, not for exploitation but for safekeeping. Protect him. Don't skim past this too quickly. In your words you have the power to protect him from criticism, to provide security for him, and to lead him to trust you implicitly.

One last word of caution: Joking has become an acceptable way to take stabs at people in our culture. We think because we were "just kidding" that no harm was done, no foul was committed. But the coarseness of our national conversation has seeped into our personal relationships. Coarse talk—rough, unrefined, callous—can cause a wound to the heart, much like a sandpaper wound on your skin—not mortal, but one that turns red and stings. Who wants to feel that? So also is any joke or silly talk that puts your husband in an uncomfortable position or in a bad light. It is not fitting, does not build up, and will soon be corrupting to his character and esteem. No good can come

Let no corrupting talk come out of your mouths, but only such as is good for building up, as fits the occasion, that it may give grace to those who hear. And do not grieve the Holy Spirit of God, by whom you were sealed for the day of redemption.

Ephesians 4:29–30

from it. You as his wife are the gallery owner who controls which images are for display, which ones are for another time, and which images must be rejected for public viewing. Only you control what others see in your husband through the lens of your words. And don't be deceived into thinking your words won't hurt if you are "just teasing." It's not just what you say publicly with others hearing, but your words matter at home with the kids and, yes, privately between just the two of you.

Be kind, my daughters. Keep your words honorable, supportive, and respectful. Always.

With deep love for each of you,
Mom

Marriage
IS LIKE
Watercolor
Painting

In high school I had a wonderful art teacher who introduced his students to watercolor painting. And it was an immediate love. Under his tutelage I developed a few basic skills, which I eagerly expanded in additional classes I took after college. But I also learned watercolor isn't very forgiving. In fact, it is considered by most to be the most difficult medium. Too much water can make the paint bleed into the wrong places and leave watermarks. Trying to cover it up with more paint creates what watercolorists call mud, because the beauty of watercolor is its transparency and luminosity, both easily lost with excess paint. The opposite problem is wind or a dry climate, which stops or inhibits the free flow of washes.

The best watercolorists learn to use these difficulties to their advantage, working with the water, letting it create interesting shapes instead of fighting it. Some have learned how to layer certain pigments, creating great depth without losing luminosity. It is an art form with the potential for exceptional beauty. Two of the best artists in this medium were John Singer Sargent and Winslow Homer. Both became skilled because they *didn't let mistakes, failures, and setbacks stop them from learning.* Their exceptional paintings are the result of years of experience.

Light shines brightest
WHEN IT IS CONTRASTED WITH DARK.

We marry for the same kind of freshness and transparent beauty found in expertly executed watercolors. But like many would-be artists who try watercolor—and find it too difficult and then quit—too many eager couples feel like giving up, or settling for mediocrity, when they don't know how to handle the challenges of the medium. God, in His grace, knows He must work to intersect our lives with circumstances beyond our control so we might learn He is God and we are not. You see, for a long while I did not understand that the light shines brightest when it is contrasted with dark. What I learned in painting, I also learned in life.

A Basic Sketch

Hi, Mom,

Are you beginning to wonder if I'm the slowest learner of all time? It seems all I have are problems and more questions. And now it seems life has gotten harder than ever. I just didn't see this coming. We started off so strong, so in love. . . . It was like the perfect, romantic ideal. And then I woke up from that dream. And he did, too. And it's, sort of, undreamy now. It's not just hard, unending work; we are bewildered. How come Disney doesn't show Cinderella and Prince Charming dealing with med school or babies who won't sleep through the night? That's what I want to know. . . . Everything's too neat and tidy and finished in the movies. And it makes me mad!

To every beautiful bride,

First of all, we are all slow learners when it comes to doing marriage God's way. I think you've heard me say that in more than one of the letters I've written you. But I'm also truly sorry it's been hard. I do wish it weren't so, but you are right that the happily-ever-after message of movies and fairy tales has created the wrong vision. Every woman has been in your shoes. No marriage is exempt from work, unexpected trials, and challenges.

Before I reply more to your question, I have to say that your weddings were such a delight to me. Parents prepare their children—and some of you are getting nearer now that you have young teens—and pray for this moment for years and years, so your weddings were in many ways gifts to both sets of parents. They were days of realizing God's provision, of seeing Him orchestrate details, and of watching Him reveal the answers to our prayers. What a celebration a wedding is, with its strong reminders of God's choosing us, His calling us His bride, His invitation to the marriage supper of the Lamb. Full of symbolism and eternal meaning, weddings call our hearts to a heavenly home.

Yes, weddings often have a magical quality—you can almost see pixie dust glittering in the air—but happily ever after is not to be found in any marriage on earth. Too many of us women have staked our hopes on finding the right guy, the right dress, and the perfect ceremony without thinking much about becoming the right person. Hundreds of hours are spent on the big day without realizing marriage itself is the event. The wedding is only day one. On day two, the real work of creating a marriage masterpiece begins. But most couples stare at the blank canvas, with no idea how to begin painting. Instead of working together to complete a basic sketch on the paper or canvas, each does his or her own thing, painting from a wide range of assumptions and beliefs. Soon the couple discovers the beautiful beginning has become clouded with muddied color because there was no plan or vision, no outline of shapes, no horizon line. In short, most newlyweds have no unified direction.

The basic sketch for every marriage is summarized in the vows you promised each other. Vows are your statements of commitment to one another. And today, the expectations for marriage are almost beyond reach because the focal point of most marriages is on *what you can or should do for me*. In our shortsightedness we want the part of the vows that say "for better, for richer, and in health." Serving each other, caring for each other, "for worse and for poorer and in sickness" is not part of the agreement anymore. We want happy paint, not a purpose or plan—which sounds so unromantic. But without a sketch or a goal, no painting succeeds and no marriage succeeds.

You are not alone in how you feel. Many a bride has left her ball dreamily walking on air, to wake up one day surrounded by piles of dirty laundry and tarnished or broken wedding gifts. And then there are little

> When you love someone you do not love them all the time, in exactly the same way, from moment to moment. It is an impossibility. It is even a lie to pretend to. And yet this is exactly what most of us demand. We have so little faith in the ebb and flow of life, of love, of relationships.
>
> —Anne Morrow Lindbergh, *Gift From the Sea*

ones—the evidence of the union she and her love have shared—but who keep her from sleep and always need her for something.

And where is Prince Charming? Isn't he supposed to come to her rescue? I'm afraid not. And that, too, is part of the problem. Every generation of women has expected too much from their husbands. We want a human savior to rescue and fix it *now*. We women expect more of our husbands than God ever intended.

Your purpose as wife is not to make him happy, nor is it his purpose to make you happy. Such a focal point is destined to fail. As you said in your email, you feel somewhat deceived by the common perception that love is easy and happiness normal. And you should. But it's a healthy discovery, an important realization to learn it takes work. Be grateful for this aha moment.

Here is the hope: The very best marriages, the ones that go the distance, have a purpose beyond mutual fulfillment and personal happiness. When I work on a painting using good tools with a sketch worked out on paper, there is potential in the end of being satisfied and even pleased with my work. It doesn't always happen, because I make mistakes, just like in marriage, but if I persevere and keep learning, and continue to try again, I have hope that I can become a decent artist. And I have greater hope that I can create a marriage masterpiece because I have the Master Artist guiding my hand surely and steadily to accomplish His purpose for the marriage He has called us to paint. In my marriage I look to Christ to give me by His Spirit all that I do not possess on my own to create my part of our marriage painting. I focus on using my femaleness as He intended when He made me for the good of my husband and our marriage. And my husband does the same. Our purpose is to keep our vows, to follow God's plan for marriage, and to do it all for His glory that others might see our painting and be encouraged to not give up and quit.

Any wedding is nothing more than the idea, the inspiration that propelled the Artist to gather the two novices, the supplies, and the tools for this particular painting. Though it will begin with a beautiful first wash of color, before the painting is complete decades in the future, there will be necessary years of skill development for these two assigned to this marriage in this place for this masterpiece.

As our friend Gary Thomas has said, marriage isn't designed to make us happy but to make us holy. Once we embrace this overarching purpose, trusting the Artist of our lives when He adds colors we don't like is a little easier. Like Michelangelo, who wrote that he suffered strained muscles and "squinting brain and eye," we must understand that creating the beauty of holiness is going to require intense work. There are no magic wands, but we do belong to a miracle-working Father!

While the joy of every wedding is a taste of heaven on earth, if we experienced that kind of joy and "perfection" many days, I doubt we'd ever want to leave this planet for heaven. We wouldn't feel a need for the Savior. But the hard truth is that life is difficult, and you are learning in new ways what Jesus said plainly: "In this world you will have trouble" (John 16:33 NIV), and "Each day has enough trouble of its own" (Matthew 6:34 NIV). He made it abundantly clear, though we are in serious denial regarding this promise, that trouble is daily, worldwide, and inevitable. Happily ever after, a life without trouble, is not our destiny. I'm glad to hear you have realized that.

- Remember, the true purpose for marriage is his and her holiness.

- Unwavering commitment is the glue that lasts a lifetime.

- Your husband is not supposed to meet all your needs.

- Your marriage is a work in progress with the best yet to come.

Ah, my beautiful Cinderellas, may you cling to Him no matter how hard life becomes.

With love for you forever,
Mom

SUFFERING WITH PERSPECTIVE

Darks and Lights

Dear Mom,

As you know from our phone chat, it feels like life is falling apart here. The job loss was bad enough, but now my washing machine isn't working and hauling baskets of clothes to a Laundromat isn't something I even have time for right now! Everything seems to be going wrong. I'm not sure how I'm supposed to build a marriage when I'm just trying to survive LIFE. And what's with God sending us all these challenges when we're trying to live for Him? I thought He'd protect us more than this, or at least not let another crisis greet me this morning. It's the last thing I need. . . .

My daughters, my friends,

I get barely surviving. That was my experience, too, more often than I would have liked. One of the most important lessons I learned when I resumed art lessons ten years ago was the importance of darks in a painting. It was a new principle for me, that the light colors stand out more dramatically when a dark or mousy color is purposely painted next to or near the bright area. The skilled use of lights and darks is what makes a master painting work, as much as its composition or subject matter does. It was hard for me to learn this concept because I was afraid I'd mess up my pretty bright colors by adding dark ones nearby, just as I was afraid in the deep recesses of my heart of God, though I would never have said so. But God is not a bit afraid to add dark to the painting of our lives, because He knows He can work rich beauty in those places. Like Job, I have learned that God allows difficult and painful times in our lives. Unanswered prayers, the death of one we love, the calamity of a tornado . . . all are from God's hand, which rules with mysterious purposes and ways. He knows with time we, too, will find treasures in the darkness. I didn't know this in the early days.

Years of lightness are what most newlyweds expect, and we were not an exception. When we moved into an adorable post-WWII cottage, painted a sunny yellow with white trim, in the summer of 1976, I didn't foresee any dark clouds on the horizon of my life. But that September, Grandpa Rainey died suddenly at the age of sixty-six; in

October and November we received two reduced pay-checks; in January 1977 Dennis returned to Missouri to run the family business for two weeks; and then Benjamin, just sixteen months old, had emergency hernia-repair surgery in April. Trying to catch our breath from all these unexpected trials, we assumed we were finished with hard times for a while. *Enough already,* we both thought.

But there was more dark paint about to be splashed on our canvas.

One June morning, after feeding our two little ones, I went back to our bedroom to do my exercise routine, still trying to get back in shape after Benjamin's birth. Suddenly feeling faint, I walked to the bed and sat down with my head on my knees. I thought I'd just stood up too fast, so I remained still, waiting for my body to calm and my head to clear. But it did not. Each time I tried to lift my head, everything tunneled into black. After only a few minutes we knew something was wrong, and Dennis called an ambulance.

An hour later I was hooked up to all kinds of wires and monitors, with doctors scrambling to figure out why my heart was beating at over three hundred beats a minute. I was in the ICU alone; Dennis was alone in the waiting area. As the day wore on, both of us became more afraid: Dennis feared he might soon be a single parent, and I feared I would die at the age of twenty-eight.

In the midst of our crisis, an invaluable gift of love was being given by a dear woman, Miz Kitty, who began to

> To put it simply, marriage is a relationship far more engrossing than we want it to be. It always turns out to be more than we bargained for. It is disturbingly intense, disruptively involving, and that is exactly the way it was designed to be. It is supposed to be more, almost, than we can handle. . . . For that is its very purpose: to get us out beyond our depth, out of the shallows of our own secure egocentricity and into the dangerous and unpredictable depths of a real interpersonal encounter.
>
> —Mike Mason, *The Mystery of Marriage*

pray nonstop. Miz Kitty prayed without ceasing for me from noon until four in the afternoon. At that precise moment she said she knew everything was okay. Either I was well or I was in heaven. She did not know until later that at four o'clock, my heart suddenly converted to a normal rhythm, just as cardiologists were walking to my room to use electric shock, which was a risky new treatment at the time.

Were we relieved? Yes, a thousand times. But were we suddenly back to normal? Hardly. Everything I believed about God had just been scrambled. The death of my father-in-law was unexpected, but a normal part of an older life. I could process that. But my own near death was not so easily assimilated. A swath of dark wet paint was brushed across our canvas, and it spread over the surface, changing every color it touched to dingy gray. We felt what Jeremiah said, "I have forgotten happiness" (Lamentations 3:17 NASB).

For the next nine months I lived with daily fear. Would it happen again? Today? Tomorrow? No one knew what had caused the extremely rapid heartbeat. I made numerous trips to doctors for tests as they tried to put a name on my condition, walking away with prescriptions for expensive meds that gave me headaches. Just accepting that I had a "condition" was a shock. I'd always assumed I was healthy. And then, though it amazes me to this day, I found myself pregnant with number three a month later. There was certainly no romance between us. We were too numb. I didn't cry or laugh or feel much of anything other than fear and anxiety that entire summer. I don't even remember making love in the month that followed our nightmare in the hospital. All of life had been reduced to simply going through the motions.

There was no joy to be found even in the initial news of another baby.

There was only more fear. Fear that this child would not be normal or survive. Fear that I would not survive another delivery. Fear stalked me like a shadow and clung to me like a leech. I wondered constantly what in the world God was doing. Why had He allowed this? I wasn't angry, only bewildered. There were no answers, only silence to my prayers asking for understanding. Dennis and I processed our fear and loss more or less alone. Yes, we talked, we listened to each other. But at its core, suffering is a lonely experience. Writer and artist Mary Anne Radmacher once said, "Sometimes courage is the quiet voice at the end of the day that says 'I will try again tomorrow.'" That was how we moved forward, one day at a time.

In the midst of it all I wrote what I was learning on a piece of notebook paper that I later found when I went through all my journals. I wrote that I understood better the truth in James 4:14, "You do not know what your life will be like tomorrow. You are just a vapor that appears for a little while and then vanishes away" (NASB). This had always been a "someday in the far distant future when I'm old" truth. Not something I'd come to understand in my twenties. I chose to believe that God would indeed bring good out of this, for He is "full of compassion and is merciful" (James 5:11 NASB). Somehow He would make that happen. I was counting on it.

God was adding lots of dark, murky paint to our canvas during the years 1976, 1977, and the first part of 1978. And it didn't feel good. I didn't like Him messing up the bright colors I preferred, the plan I had in mind for my life and family. In March 1978 I survived the healthy birth of Samuel. We were enormously relieved. His arrival returned us to a more normal kind of living, with more ordinary stresses of three children age four and under. With no additional heart episodes, I was finally beginning to relax. With great relief, we could begin to relegate those challenging years to past tense. Later, we'd come to understand that suffering and struggle are just part of life. It comes to us all, for some

rarely but suddenly, for others as a constant, tidal shift. And we learned there's always a reason for it, even if we never know what it is.

Though a near-death experience was not in my plans, it was in God's. It was a significant lesson in understanding that God owes me nothing for my attempts to live for Him. My inaccurate beliefs about what to expect from God—I call it fairy-tale theology—were failing me, but God was graciously replacing it with bedrock truth. As God responded to Job, He gave me no reasons for why He knit me in my mother's womb with a heart defect, nor did He apologize for those especially challenging years of suffering. I was like a child before Him, clueless before my Parent, yet in His grace willing to trust and not reject His sovereign rule over my life. I remained "perplexed, but not despairing" (2 Corinthians 4:8 NASB).

Even without a major life-and-death crisis, each day is lived with the suffering and trials of sin's effects in family relationships. The more selfish people in your household, the more conflict and relational stresses you will

happy ending

God will use hardship to fashion beauty in our lives
and marriages. The happy ending we long for comes
on the road of suffering, not the road of ease.

experience. Simple multiplication makes that clear. But the key is to submit it all to Him, to accept the darks in the midst of the light, and to seek to see how those colors, too, can draw us closer to Him.

You, too, will experience seasons of trial and suffering. They are a normal part of marriage from beginning to end. "Do not be surprised," said Peter, "at the fiery ordeal . . . as though some strange thing were happening" (1 Peter 4:12 NASB). And said James to all who will listen, "Consider it all joy . . . when you encounter various trials" (James 1:2 NASB).

I wish there were another way to be made more like Jesus. But truly, this is the paradox of His work in our world . . . through pain, through the sorrows of loss, we can become closer to Him. Just as dark shadows anchor objects in a painting, so our shadowed experiences of His strife, His struggles, His sacrifice secure us to the One who is unchanging.

Remember, no hardship or suffering comes to God's children without His permission, His will. He wants to use it to fashion beauty in our lives and marriages. The happy ending we long for comes on the road of suffering, not the road of ease. Now, "to him who is able to keep you from stumbling and to present you before his glorious presence without fault and with great joy" (Jude 1:24 NIV). Amen.

- Though the darks may scare you, cling to Jesus through it all.

- He will never leave you or forsake you. Count on it.

- He knows the number of days that were ordained for you.

Yours for a deepening bedrock faith in the years when God picks up the paintbrush loaded with darks,

Love,
Mom

Perspective and Focal Point

Dear Mom,

I love my man. I'm thankful for him. Most—MOST—every day. But Mom, our relationship seems to be so much harder than other people's. I just don't understand. It's like we are on autopilot, just going through the motions. Honestly, it feels like God sometimes really does give us more than we can handle. And I just don't think what I've been dealt is entirely fair. I'm trying to live a good life, one that honors Him. Why doesn't He honor me in that? Or at least give me a sense that He is with me in the middle of it all?

To my creative girls (all of you, yes, all of you!),

In the years when getting to church on time was a major event every week, maybe even before Laura was born, I remember a specific family in our church who seemed to arrive peacefully, happily, and all put together. Never mind that she only had three kids to get ready while I had five—or was it six? Regardless, my perspective was that the children were adorable, always dressed beautifully, not in hand-me-downs or garage-sale finds like ours. The mom was tall and thin and always dressed attractively. You relate already, don't you? From my vantage across the aisle, it seemed they never struggled with the stuff we dealt with, like learning disabilities, health issues, sibling rivalry, or ordinary marriage struggles. Because we weren't friends, just acquaintances, I never saw behind the polished Sunday morning exterior. I knew they were as broken as we, but sometimes it was hard not to compare my known reality with what I

thought was their reality. Life feels unfair any time we let our eyes view a couple's canvas from afar.

We women all battle this temptation: comparison. Sadly, it doesn't stop with age, but I don't care as much as I used to, and that is a great victory! Comparison or perspective is another principle I learned in my art classes. Creating depth on a flat, one-dimensional surface necessitates mimicking what our eyes see in nature on a horizontal plane. Trees in the distance appear smaller and bluer than they actually are, so they must be painted smaller and in muted greens on the canvas. They aren't the focal point, but the background or supporting cast. The family in our church was simply part of the background of my life. My problem was I wanted my painting, the colors God had given me to work with, to look more like theirs. Sometimes I focused too much on what was around me instead of the focal point of my marriage and my family.

The Master Artist not only has a plan and a purpose for your marriage, but He has a vantage point, a perspective that you simply do not have. His view of our lives is total, knowing from beginning to end. His all-knowing mind chooses to give precisely what is needed at the right time. Remember, He makes no mistakes. When He is busily adding layers and muted colors that don't make sense to us, from His perspective He is adding depth and richness. I didn't appreciate His giving us trials, but instead wanted a smooth ride and thought this other family had that kind of life.

Once again I return to the theme of mystery in this letter, for the execution of this work of art called marriage cannot be achieved without surrendering faith, nor can it succeed if our eyes are on others instead of Him. Fixing our eyes on Jesus is my need. Gazing at others changes perspective and invites discouragement. We see from afar what appear to be happy, healthy people, strong marriages, and well-behaved children . . . and we assume God is not working muted paint in their lives like He is in ours. Just as viewing a small painting in a museum from across the room blurs the detail and nuanced contrasts that are foundational, so does viewing other marriages and other families from a distance give a fuzzy picture.

Comparison is a subtle but debilitating temptation for both men and women, and it can lead to jealousy, anger, resentment, and even rejecting God Himself. I remember a children's book in which a little monkey was working on a painting. He admired what the other animal artists were painting and asked for their help. Each came with his brush and added a new element to the monkey's painting. The result was an ugly mess. The moral of the story is the little monkey needed to paint his own vision and not try to be like everyone else. God is saying, "Paint with the colors and vision I give you. Trust me."

A favorite writer of mine, Andrée Seu Peterson, wrote about playing the hand you are dealt in life, acknowledging God, who gives and takes away, and continuing to believe each day by faith. She wrote, "To believe in Christ, in this moment, in this perplexity, in this frustration, in these setbacks, in this present agony, is victory of the highest order." The strongest women, the strongest wives, trust the sovereign Creator in all seasons, in all circumstances, and with all God gives. These women keep believing His goodness because "this is the victory that has overcome the world—our faith" (1 John 5:4). We mistakenly believe it is the miracle or the answered prayer that overcomes in victory; instead it is unwavering faith in the face of ongoing frustration and struggles. Steadfast faith is the real miracle. And steadfast faith produces strength.

You have been given a difficult circumstance. It is not to see how much you can bear, but so that you can experience His sustaining strength holding you up. Even when the circumstance is not yours, but a dear friend's, like the many you know who have walked away from their marriages and their faith, even then He wants you to run to Him and keep your eyes on Him. Understanding how someone who walked the walk and even taught others to follow Christ could change so dramatically, rejecting all he or she once believed, may never be answered satisfactorily this side of heaven, but at some point a decision was made that Christ couldn't help them and the faith door was closed. Keep following Jesus and keep His Word as your focal point, and this will never be your story.

One of my favorite verses is Luke 1:37, "For nothing will be impossible with God." No circumstance, no spouse, no child, no in-laws, no job, no relationship or tragedy is too hard for God. And what I also love is that

Marriage is a way not to evade suffering, but to suffer purposefully.

—Mike Mason, *The Mystery of Marriage*

God made this same statement at least seven other times, a reminder for every day of the week plus an extra of His power over all:

"Is anything too hard for the Lord?" Genesis 18:14

"I know that you can do all things." Job 42:2

"Nothing is too hard for you." Jeremiah 32:17

"Is anything too hard for me?" Jeremiah 32:27

"With man this is impossible, but with God all things are possible." Matthew 19:26

"Abba, Father, all things are possible for you." Mark 14:36

"The things that are impossible with people are possible with God." Luke 18:27 NASB

So keep your eyes where they belong. On Jesus. Not on others.

How do we respond when God doesn't heal a grave sickness or save a life—as He did not save our sweet granddaughter Molly, though we all prayed each day of her short life for a miracle? What are we to think when He doesn't intervene to stop evil from harming an innocent child? Can He be trusted when my husband and I argue for the thousandth time about the same thing? How does He allow a spouse to hurt another? We don't understand and perhaps never will, but I do know God can still be trusted and believed, and that one day we will see clearly. His character never changes. But when God doesn't change those hard places in your marriage, in your husband, in your circumstances, will you continue to believe? That is the ultimate question.

Seasons of plenty lead us to relax. That's not wrong, or bad—we all need some relief—but we can get lulled into a sense of complacency. We forget to be alert. Too much comfort can leave us vulnerable. We might be more easily deceived, more easily caught off guard by trouble or by ordinary difficulties. In fairy tales, it is when all is well that the evil king attacks. The true warrior on alert is always at the ready.

> *Too much comfort can leave us vulnerable — more easily deceived, more easily caught off guard by trouble or by ordinary difficulties.*

The great hope I offer you is that the fight for your marriage is worth it. Whether the contrasts and clashes in your marriage are from sin or from circumstances beyond your control, God wants to use them to produce "the peaceful fruit of righteousness . . . that we may share his holiness" (Hebrews 12:11, 10). Our friend Jerry Sittser says in his book *A Grace Disguised* that the tragedy or loss is not as important as our response to that loss. I hope you don't miss that. This man who lost his wife, his daughter, and his mother in a tragic accident said *our response is more important than the loss or the difficulty itself*. A radical way of thinking, true, but it is crucial to growing strong faith.

- There are treasures to be found in the darkness of struggle, but only by those with the eyes of faith.

- Diligently reject the comparison trap.

- Remember God's design for you, and your marriage will be unlike any other.

- Give thanks and rejoice in those uniquenesses instead of resenting them.

May you have eyes to see the Unseen,
Mom

P.S. I need to say, I am not naïve about some of the terribly difficult circumstances in some marriages today. Dennis and I know of marriages that are crashing because a spouse is a narcissist, a sex addict, or a pathological liar, is choosing a same-sex lifestyle, or has a completely closed heart to change. In addition, many men appear to be using the Christian cloak for selfish advantage but are not following Christ as Lord. I do not condemn women who make decisions to create distance from these men for their own protection and that of their children. I strongly encourage these women to seek the protection and wisdom of their church and/or a godly counselor before reuniting with men who are choosing a sinful lifestyle.

Yes, God delights in redemption and restoration, but He must have the canvas of individual hearts surrendered to Him on which to work. For you or any friend, decisions to leave and ultimately divorce must be made carefully with abundant wise counsel guided closely by the Bible. When holiness is the goal, God will supply all that you or anyone will need to continue to trust Him step-by-step. In time He will work His wonders. But when happiness is the goal, escape is the only sensible option. No miracles will be seen.

It is a deep grief to see marriages end, and worse, the ripple effects are greater than most imagine. The significant rise in repeated divorces in the last several decades is producing young men and women who haven't a clue how to be men and women or how to be married. They have no model, and they are wounded. We are reaping the results in your generation. My greatest desire is that you, and other women and men, will choose to believe God no matter what hand you've been dealt. The Bible is full of supernatural stories, but the angel appearances, the multiplied oil, the miraculous victories only occurred when God's people were at the end of their rope but still full of faith. May it be so of you.

Making a Collage

During the years I was taking watercolor classes, some of the most creative and fun classes happened when we came with our old discarded paintings that were either incomplete or just plain terrible and a bag full of craft tools like scissors, shaped hole punches, and glitter. For hours we'd sit at a Ping-Pong table and cut and tear those mediocre watercolors into interesting shapes. Watercolor paper tears with frayed, deckled edges, which create a nice effect when layered. Rough edges can be beautiful. From all the old castoffs, new works of art emerged. We all oohed and ahhed over one another's efforts.

Isn't creating a collage with the torn and incomplete fragments a picture of life? One of the attributes of my God that I love most is His great love for redemption. He delights in taking the broken and damaged and giving it new life. In fact, He seems to take special joy in resurrecting what we would consider the most unworthy.

Which means that no sin is beyond His healing. No spouse is too hard for Him to soften. No marriage is too ugly for Him to make beautiful. Even blended marriages with their challenging complexities can make the most interesting and fascinating collages of all. And isn't that worth shouting about? Isn't this truth worth singing about? When I think of how much God loves to redeem it all—everything in our lives and hearts—it makes me want to cheer as if I were in a stadium with thousands on their feet,

arms raised in victory. But it also makes me want to bow in worship. That God would redeem me, one so unworthy, so broken, so full of weakness and propensity to sin, is truly overwhelming. No wonder those in the Bible who literally saw visions of God fell flat on their faces. When we see Him as He is, we are left awed and speechless.

As you continue painting your marriage, you'll develop a whole gallery full of work. There will be those days and weeks when it seems you have left nothing but mud on your fine watercolor paper, far from frame worthy. It makes no sense in the moment why your good intentions didn't work, or why your sincere efforts to create beauty fell flat. Set the day's work aside, but don't stop believing. God isn't finished. One day He will redeem those hours, those days, those months, those years . . . and in the process reveal a new use for those seemingly scrapped pieces in the collage of your marriage.

Not long after Molly died, a friend sent us this quote from the book *The North Face of God* by Ken Gire (emphasis added).

The darkness strips us of our keys, our formulas, our techniques. It takes them and tosses them down the side of the mountain. And though we feel we can't make the climb without them, the truth is that they were some of the very things that weighed us down and held us back. . . . And as we wait, we pray. *Our prayers may not hurry the sun, but they will heighten our awareness to what is happening in the darkness.* As incongruous as it seems, sacred things happen there. C. S. Lewis noted the paradox when he asked, "Why are so many holy places dark places?" They are holy because, even in the dark of night and the cold of March, God is at work, breaking through the husk around our hearts and bringing life from under the dead leaves.

God is always at work, stripping away the things we think are so important to life. He knows they are dangerous distractions from Him. We don't like the dark places or the places of stark contrast. We want light and happiness. And God does, too. But He knows we look in all the wrong places. So trust Him, knowing the hard places are sacred places if we will believe.

My desire is that you, too, will overcome through the suffering of your life. Don't listen to the enemy, who will whisper words of fear to you. Remember, it is all about trusting His composition, accepting the colors He adds, all while continuing to believe.

- No matter what God brings your way, I pray you will say with Job, "Though He slay me, yet will I trust Him" (13:15 NKJV).

- Your life is a painting. Trust God's brushstrokes.

- Marriage is a collage of many paintings. Trust the darks and mix them with lots of lights and a generous sprinkle of glitter.

- And remember . . . faith is the glue that holds it all together.

Mom

P.S. For you daughters of Eve not in our family, Rebecca and I want to share with you a wonderful little epitaph. In the fall of 2003, after taking Laura to college and getting her all situated in her dorm room, Dennis and I went on a trip to celebrate our graduation from full-time parenthood. It had been twenty-eight years since we'd lived just the two of us, and to inaugurate this new beginning, we used our frequent-flier miles and went to England. One day while touring the southwest peninsula, we happened upon a tiny hamlet, St. Buryan. Like most old towns, it had an ancient-looking church with gravestones in the yard, all surrounded by a stone wall. We parked and wandered to the church for a peek inside, and then meandered among the gravestones. There I found a tall granite slab upon which was written the names John and Mary Wallis and Baby John; the dates of death, 1820 and 1821; and below the names this inscription:

We cannot Lord
Thy purpose see,
But all is well,
That's done by Thee

The words spoke to me, for we were in the midst of a trial unrelated to taking Laura to college. I photographed the stone and wrote the words on a scrap of paper. Almost five years later, Rebecca and her husband, Jacob, had those same words inscribed on the stone they purchased for their baby girl's tombstone. Molly was a beautiful full-term baby whose days numbered only seven. We still do not know why, but we know with confidence, all is well that's done by thee.

Rebecca and I wrote a book about the story of Molly's short life. It was a week of great heartache and profound mystery. So many young women experience miscarriages it seems, and others lose babies as Rebecca and Jake did. Rebecca's words in *A Symphony in the Dark* have brought comfort to many young women like her who are also facing grief.

> My hope is built on nothing less than Jesus' blood and righteousness; I dare not trust the sweetest frame, but wholly lean on Jesus' name.
>
> —Edward Mote, "The Solid Rock"

Marriage is for Ever After

CHAPTER 9

There was a time, long, long ago, when skies were always blue. Peace was the rule and no one knew pain. You see, we *were* created to live happily ever after. A life without thorns and thistles, loss and grief, was the original intention. In an unspoiled garden we would have seen clearly, believed fully, trusted completely. It would indeed have been as He intended, a paradise on earth.

You and I know very well our lives and our marriages are not lived in paradise. But if you've read all my letters to this point, you also know there is great hope, not just for today in this broken world but for ever after. The Bible begins with the marriage of Adam and Eve, and it ends with the marriage of the Lamb and His bride, the church. We who are the children of God will one day experience a perfect marriage inaugurated by a grand feast, and we will be dressed in pure white linen sparkling in the Light. There will be no more death or crying or loss. And the lion will lie down with the lamb.

Marriage is more than your love for each other. It has a higher dignity and power, for it is God's holy ordinance, through which he wills to perpetuate the human race till the end of time. In your love you see only your two selves in the world, but in marriage you are a link in the chain of the generations, which God causes to come and to pass away to his glory, and calls into his kingdom.

—Dietrich Bonhoeffer

In the first letter I wrote about Mako's grand and glorious painting, how he had a vision for the whole even as he worked on individual parts. Though the same must be true for us in our marriages, sadly today, we too easily lose sight of that early vision for the beauty of God's design. Couples enter marriage with the highest of hopes, certain that their love is the greatest to ever exist on the planet, only to find themselves all too quickly on the defensive, foundering in a sea of unexpected disappointments. We have lost our way because we have lost our sight.

It's as if an earthquake shook the Louvre in Paris, and half of the works of art have fallen to the floor and lie there damaged and torn and crushed. Couples arrive at the entrance, buy tickets, and begin their tour, but all they can see is the destruction, the loss. They are unable to see the beauty of what is still on display because they cannot stop looking at the magnitude of what has been destroyed. And so is the condition of marriage in this generation. Too many feel it is hopeless because the fallen marriages all around take our eyes off the original design, which still works.

The Master crafted us as men and women, each unique halves to be joined in marriage for triumph and delight, not for failure and heartache. He executed His great work

there is pain and struggle in the process but always there is the hope of redemption and worth and beauty as we persevere until the end.

of art with love for our welfare. But unlike most great artists and their paintings, God has left His unfinished. He has given us the foundational structural elements, like tubes of paint with color names on them: love, help, lead, respect, sacrifice, serve, protect, understand, submit, love. I have a set of basic colors, and my husband has a set. Then God hands us the brushes to paint with abandon—I mix my pigments and he mixes his, occasionally borrowing from one another; together we create a painting unique to us, continuing what He began.

Though every marriage will have a unique look, a distinct style apart from all others, every marriage should reflect God's written purposes for men and women, just as God the Father, Son, and Holy Spirit also have unique roles. Marriage, after all, is a picture of our relationship with Christ, He our leader, we His bride.

Because God didn't make us computer-animated robots, but instead gave us a free will, His desire is for us to be cocreators with Him in His vision for our marriage masterpiece. By carefully mixing pigments, boldly choosing new flavors, capturing moments of light, patiently tending what's been planted, writing a symphony, we use the gifts He's given in cooperation with His plan and purpose. Thankfully, as we work on one panel at a time, God the Master has His eye on the whole, the big picture. Yes, there is pain and struggle in the process, in this most intimate of relationships, but always there is the hope of redemption and worth and beauty as we persevere until the end.

Even more than hope is the expectation of joy in marriage. Just as there is great joy in the relationship of the Trinity—another profound mystery, living together in perfect harmony, executing their roles in perfect order so that they are always One, always in perfect unity—our marriages were intended to reflect a sparkle of that joy of oneness. That is the reward for the work of marriage, the endurance required, the forgiving, serving, helping of one another in love: the gift of sweet joy.

And the good news for you, my daughters, and for anyone else who might read these letters, is that an engraved invitation awaits from the One who will make all things right. He is ever holding out His pierced hand in welcome, promising to all who receive Him that He will never leave or abandon. The Creator says, "Come to me." It is a decision that begins in a moment of surrender and continues with an everyday following until we are called home. Faith is the key to the doorway of eternal life.

During the years of the wars in Afghanistan and Iraq, we became used to seeing features on the news from reporters who were "embedded" with the active-duty troops. In a similar way, God has embedded the institution of marriage into every culture in every generation to be a living report regarding the real truth about Himself. We are ambassadors, messengers, containers of the Holy Spirit, and yes, artists, too, deposited in every community around the world. Even less-than-ideal marriages (not wicked or abusive marriages) have a profoundly stabilizing influence on each culture. God's intent has not changed. His plans will not be manipulated. Marriages embedded in cultures are still His first line of defense against the forces of evil. And even though our culture is trying desperately to change the shape and form of marriage, His truth will not change.

Our friend Andrew Peterson, a singer and songwriter, wrote a song, "Dancing in the Minefields," that captures the radical abandon and other-worldly joy to be found in a marriage led by the Maker.

> 'Cause we bear the light of the Son of Man
> So there's nothing left to fear
> So I'll walk with you in the shadowlands
> Till the shadows disappear

May God bless you with discomfort at easy answers, half truths, and superficial relationships so that you may live deep within your heart. May God bless you with anger at injustice, oppression, and exploitation of people, so that you may wish for justice, freedom, and peace. May God bless you with enough foolishness to believe that you can make a difference in this world, so that you can do what others claim cannot be done.

—A Franciscan blessing

'Cause he promised not to leave us
And his promises are true
So in the face of all this chaos, baby,
I can dance with you.

Let's go dancing in the minefields
And sailing in the storms
This is harder than we dreamed
But I believe that's what the promises are for.

"Till death do us part" Dennis and I each repeated with sincerity, fervor, and passion on our wedding day. There were days and seasons when we weren't sure we'd survive the minefields. It was harder than we dreamed. Much harder. But our mutual decision to never give up, to end every fight or disagreement with a restatement of our promises to never leave and with a restatement of our faith in the God who is able, kept us in the dance in spite of our circumstances and feelings. Because of this commitment our vision remained, dim at times, but never extinguished.

Endurance is such an unromantic word. It sounds upside-down and backward to imply endurance produces happiness, but such is the way God works. It is where we are in our marriage today, and it is truly wonderful. The happiness we experience is more aptly described as contentment or satisfaction or peace. It is deep and lasting as opposed to the shallowness of our early years. Knowing the high purpose for which God created marriage strengthened our faith to persevere through the normal, common trials of building a healthy marriage.

May you follow Him faithfully until the end as you and your husband go dancing in the minefields of this shadowland. Never give up. That's what the promises are for!

I love all of you girls more than I can say,
Mom

Among the many titles women wear, **Barbara Rainey**'s favorites are wife, mom, Mimi, and friend.

She is married to her best friend, Dennis Rainey, whose heart has belonged to Jesus Christ since their first meeting when she was a sophomore and he a junior in college. Her six children are all adults who amaze her with the ways they are using their abilities and gifts to live for Christ. And from five of these six have come twenty-two grandchildren who call her Mimi. But the best title of all is to be called friend by Jesus. Barbara is increasingly in awe at being chosen and loved by Him.

In addition to these most important relationships are the titles artist, author, and ambassador, which tell more about what Barbara loves to do. She joined the staff of Cru right out of college and married Dennis in 1972, and together they started FamilyLife, a ministry of Cru, in 1976 with two other couples in a tiny little office in Little Rock, Arkansas. Together, Barbara and Dennis have sought to be living witnesses for the King.

Over the years, she has learned to speak at Weekend to Remember marriage conferences and continues to be a frequent guest on *FamilyLife Today*, a nationally syndicated radio program. As her children began to leave home for college, she resumed art lessons and began growing as an author. She coauthored a number of books with her husband and wrote several herself.

More recently, Barbara has begun a new venture within FamilyLife called Ever Thine Home, a holiday and home collection of beautiful and biblical products for women to use to make their homes a witness for their faith.

And since this is the ending page of a book on marriage, Barbara wants to strongly encourage every reader to continue to invest in her marriage by using all that FamilyLife has to offer: the Weekend to Remember marriage getaways, the Art of Marriage events, the *FamilyLife Today* daily radio broadcast, and downloadable podcasts on every topic imaginable to strengthen your marriage and family.

To learn more about Ever Thine Home and FamilyLife, read the blogs, subscribe to updates, and more, visit them online:

everthinehome.com

familylife.com

JOIN A SMALL GROUP BIBLE STUDY

On both websites you will find a free book study with questions that will facilitate small-group discussions on each of the nine chapters in this book. We hope you will join other wives in conversations encouraging one another to grow in the art of becoming a godly wife.

Barbara would love to hear from you. Write her at everthinehome.com.